DETOUR

My Cancer Journey

Dear Joan & Dave,
You have no idea the impact you both had on my young life. Christ is evident in your countenance and your everyday life. Whenever I think of you, I thank God that He sent you to the little town of Oxford Maine and that He blessed us with your wisdom and enthusiasm!
Though miles have separated us, the bond we have in Him keeps us together.
I hope this humble story will bring even a little bit of encouragement.

Terri L. Wakefield

Love,
Terri

ISBN 978-1-64299-351-6 (paperback)
ISBN 978-1-64299-352-3 (digital)

Christian Faith Publishing, Inc.
832 Park Avenue
Meadville, PA 16335
www.christianfaithpublishing.com

Printed in the United States of America

Dedication

Wholeheartedly this book is dedicated first and foremost to the One and Only Jesus Christ, who not only is my Lord, my Savior, but my very personal friend who was always near, always encouraging and always guiding. Without You, this book would not have happened. I pray that you will use this to encourage just 1 other person in the struggles they may face and that they will see that You are the answer to all of life's struggles.

I also want to dedicate this book to 5 people whose love and friendship got me through dark days: To my daughters Casandra and Heather for sacrificing their time and interrupting their lives to be there day in and day out to care for me, even at my worst, and loving me through it all. To Toby, my son, for being available whenever I needed him for whatever I needed him for. To my late husband Keith, whose love surpassed physical appearance and emotional ups and downs with unwavering support.

To my very best friend in the whole wide world, Patty Hodgdon. Your friendship, love, and support saw me through some dark days, and I knew I could always count on you to give it to me straight whether I wanted to hear it or not. You mean so very much to me.

Acknowledgements

First, I want to thank my very good friend Carrie Boatman for editing my first draft of this work. She pushed and prodded when I needed it and encouraged me throughout the process. Her input was invaluable and her friendship even more precious.

Secondly, I want to thank my second-look editor Mary Delameter, whose eye for detail surpasses even the best editors and who put an excellent finishing shine to this book.

Thirdly, I want to say thank you to all the people in my life who encouraged me to continue on when I felt too discouraged to open another computer word document and push my brain to remember feelings and emotions and facts and events that sometimes felt good to push away. You all have been the rainbows on cloudy days that have given me hope and ignited the energy to persevere and to continue a journey I often felt too tired to continue on.

Chapter 1

The Beginning

August 15, 2011

It was a beautiful August day in 2011. My daughters and I decided to head to the city to choose some eyeglasses for me. We had lunch and did some more shopping. On the way home, I called the doctor's office to check on a biopsy my husband, Keith, had on a lump on the top of his head and to check on a breast needle biopsy I had had done the week before. The office personnel told me that Keith's biopsy was clean and that there was nothing to worry about. Apparently, his biopsy results were handy. Mine, on the other hand, seemed to have arrived but were "not available" at the time of my call.

"They are probably just in the doctor's inbox, but she is off today. I'm sure she will call you with the results when she reviews them tomorrow," her staff informed me.

I generally allow the doctor's office to call me with test results, but I was a bit anxious to hear about both of these biopsies and decided I would call. My husband is so dear to me that the thought of something happening to him was hard to bear. I told the girls that nothing serious ever happens to me physically, and so, I was not really worried about my results. In the back of my mind, though, I knew there was the possibility of something more serious from some of the wording used by the radiologist the day of my biopsy.

About a month or so earlier, at an annual physical exam, my primary-care physician convinced me to get my mammogram done. It had been a couple of years—a recommendation that my physician in Arizona said was usually a safe option. It was a few months past the two-year mark, and my primary-care physician insisted I get it done as soon as possible. I made the arrangements and went in for the mammogram. I really dislike having it done, as most people do. Not only is it a little (or a lot) uncomfortable to have the breast compressed as much as one can stand by this clear plastic square paddle that gets cranked down onto the breast that has been awkwardly maneuvered onto a shelf that holds the film, but it is also a bit embarrassing to have someone you are not married to handling such an intimate part of the body.

I am not a prude, and so, I put on my best face and made it through, thanking the Lord that he has given knowledge to the healthcare professionals and that he is directing the course of events. It is easy to be rational when the possible outcome has not yet happened. I was glad to have this "unnecessary" interruption to my normal routine over and done with and went on with the rest of my day.

It is at times like this, though, when I wish I had more of my mother's personality. She would have been able to rise above the uncomfortable circumstances and jest with the personnel, make some joke about getting her "boob" squeezed, and been otherwise a very memorable patient. I, on the other hand, am more like my dad, quiet and composed, a *shrinking violet* one might say, and my awkward attempts at humor are often embarrassingly bad.

I needed to get home and go to bed. You see, at this time, I worked from midnight to 8:00 a.m. at home doing quality assurance for a national medical transcription service. My job was to review medical reports dictated by healthcare professionals that have been transcribed/edited by healthcare documentation specialists but that have questions they were not able to resolve. They send them to the QA specialists (proofreaders is another word to describe us) for a word that could not be understood or a term they are not familiar with, patient information that could not be found, or some other issue that could compromise patient safety and care and therefore could not be uploaded directly to the client (hospital or clinic usually). Because of my background, I am well versed in medical terminology, anatomy and physiology, drug nomenclature, diagnostic tests, disease processes, and quickly researching new terms that seem to become part of the language of medicine overnight. This knowledge can be quite useful when the healthcare providers start using terms that can scare you if you don't know what they mean. But, it can also be a hindrance when you start to think you know more than the doctor does, and I have to admit there are times…

After I arrived home from the mammogram, the radiology department of the local hospital called to say that something showed up on the mammogram, and they needed to take more views. They asked me if I could come back in the next day or two to get that done. *Okay, first red flag.*

Maybe that wasn't an unnecessary inconvenience after all. I have had "densities" in the past and have had fibrocystic breast disease, which is a fancy name for dense, lumpy breasts that things like caffeine can aggravate. I drink a little caffeine by the way—okay, a lot of caffeine. I made arrangements to go back in two days.

More views were done, and those were reviewed while I waited. Because the right breast masses—yes, two masses—were still visible, they wanted to do a breast ultrasound while I was still in the department because a tech was available. *Okay, second red flag: two masses.*

They put the mammogram films up on the light board, so I could see the suspicious areas. Yep, there they are, lighting up the film like asymmetrical headlights. All right, let's move on to the ultrasound, so we can find out they are really nothing to be concerned about. The tech does his thing, moving the wand back and forth across the skin, watching the screen as it shows the area in question, taking measurements, and trying to see if anything shows up within the mass, like debris or a septation, for instance, and then the radiologist reviews the results.

The radiologist came in and let me know that I have two solid structures in the right breast, very close to each other, at the 9:30

and 10:30 o'clock positions. The larger of the two is around 1.5 cm, which they assure me is small. They are not cysts. He said that my options are to follow up at six-month intervals (he would be comfortable with this option if I was his wife or daughter, he tells me), an MRI, which insurance will not pay for, or a biopsy. I could not imagine waiting six months to see "what happens." I can't afford to pay for an MRI myself. The only other option is to have the biopsy.

Fortunately, they could do it immediately. Because I have generally downplayed what might be momentous negative events in my life, in hindsight, I believe I was rationalizing again that this was going to turn out to be nothing. After getting approval from my primary caregiver's office, they get ready to do the biopsy, and I sit in the waiting room watching Rachael Ray's TV show. *"Boy, that looks good,"* I'm thinking. *"I'll have to get online and get that recipe."*

"Terri, we're ready for you," the caregiver said. My cooking plans are quickly forgotten as I am now ushered to a different ultrasound room that is set up to do biopsies. I am praying, *"Lord, I am getting a bit anxious about these circumstances."*

I had called one of my daughters who lives close by to let her know what was happening, and she offered to come, but it "isn't a big deal," I tell her. I guess this was my way of minimizing just how critical this biopsy might be. If I say it isn't a big deal, then it won't be, right? Besides I have my best friend with me so I am never truly alone, and he is helping my heart stay relatively calm under the circumstances. My tendency to take things moment by moment sometimes hinders my seeing that though at the moment I am feeling okay about what is going on, that might change as the current situation progresses. Though I am not sure that this thought was conscious, did I want my daughter to hear the words that I might have cancer when I probably wasn't ready to hear them myself? I forget that having someone close, who you can touch and who you can share spoken and unspoken thoughts with, is something God himself ordained and encouraged.

As the radiologist came into the room, my thoughts switched to what is physically going to happen to my body in the next few minutes. Will it hurt? Can't you just put me out? You see, I am a real wimp when it comes to physical pain.

They administer a local anesthetic and take two samples of the first lesion and place a "clip" so they can see the spot later. They then take two samples of the other lesion and place another clip. As the radiologist and the ultrasound tech are discussing positions and where to stick the needle, I hear "cancer" being used in a "what if" scenario. Even with the local anesthesia, there was a significant amount of pressure and maneuvering that left some black and blue areas; however, it wasn't too painful and a small price to pay for knowing sooner what may be going on. They informed me that I would probably not get the results until the following week.

So now we wait…

"Terri, this is Dr. Latkovich…"

I am taken aback as this call came in about five minutes after I had called her office for the results and was informed it was her day off. Okay, *big* red flag: Doctors don't call you at home on their day off unless it is important. She went on to explain that the biopsy was positive for invasive breast cancer. She apologized for calling me on the phone with the news rather than having me come into her office; however, she felt that I would worry more waiting for a visit than just to let me know.

I agreed and am glad that she chose to do it that way. I was sitting in my car in my daughter Cassie's driveway. Heather, my other daughter, was in the car with me when the call came in. She could tell by my voice and my thumbs down sign to her that there was a problem.

She rushed inside to get Cassie, and they both came back to the car. Their reaction was one of disbelief that the doctor would tell me such news over the phone. I assured them I was not upset about that. They were in shock, too, and obviously had questions brewing in their minds about all of it—perhaps whether I was going to die, how far along was the cancer, and all the types of questions we have when hearing news like this.

On the way home, after dropping Heather off at her apartment, I pulled off into a rest area near beautiful Lake Pennesseewassee and called my husband, Keith. I gave him the good news about his biopsy and then gave him the not-so-good news about mine. He worked as a truck driver and was on the road for one to two weeks at a time, sometimes even longer. I could not wait until he was home to tell him. I needed to tell my husband; I needed his love, his care, his compassion, and his voice.

Though it was the first that I had allowed myself to cry, the call had a calming effect on me. The rest of the ride home was a blur. My mind was caught up in the absolute truth—that God loved me, and I was safe in his care no matter what that ultimately looked like, but I was also reeling in the emotion of what was going on and what the future might hold, stirrings based on worry about whether I would be able to work. Will I need a mastectomy? Will I need chemotherapy and radiation therapy? Will I lose my hair if I do? Am I going to die from this? What will happen to my husband and kids—will they be okay? In a nutshell, I was overwhelmed.

Even though it was hard to hear, I know that God had prepared my heart for the news. You see, he has been preparing me through all of my life's experiences and through my relationship with him. I know that I can trust him with whatever comes my way. If he has chosen to allow this circumstance, then there is a purpose, and whatever that purpose is will be for his glory and for my ultimate good. Yes, I had the faith to endure the journey, but I knew that this was going to be a long, sometimes painful ride that I would need to take day by day and sometimes moment by moment.

Sort of like when you are out riding around on a beautiful fall day. You see a dirt road, and it invites you to explore its secrets. The scenery is awesome, a jumble of vivid and muted colors and shapes, but your body is jarred by the bumps, the pot holes, the tree roots and rocks that have emerged after years of exposure to the elements, often distracting you from the uniqueness of the surrounding habitat. But wait, what is that? Up ahead you see a sight that will either make you laugh or make you cry or maybe both. Leisurely crossing the path is a mother duck with her duckling brood waddling after her. The painful juts are forgotten.

Oh, to experience that kind of blind trust and innocence again. I am reminded that even in the difficult times, there is beauty and surprise in unforeseen places and a reason to venture along, trusting the one who leads us, and embracing the ups and downs of the excursion.

> *"Though he slay me, yet will I trust him"*
> *(Job 13:15).*

Social Media Posts and Emails

08.15.11—Email: Praise the Lord that Keith's skin biopsies were benign. No follow-up needed.

Praise the Lord also that God has something special he will be doing in Terri's life as her breast biopsy was positive for breast cancer. Follow-up appointment with oncologist (cancer specialist) next week. Will keep you updated. I would be happy to speak with anyone who is willing to share any personal experience with this. Feel free to contact me via email or my cell number.

Praise the Lord for he is good and faithful, beyond our imaginations!

08.21.11—"Actually, I don't have a sense of needing anything personally. I've learned by now to be quite content whatever my circumstances. I'm just as happy with little as with much, with much as with little. I've found the recipe for being happy whether full or hungry, hands full or hands empty. Whatever I have, wherever I am, I can make it through anything in the one who makes me who I am." ~ Philippians 4:9–11 (The Message).

08.22.11—I want to thank everyone for their well wishes and prayers. I really covet the prayers. Oncologist appt on Wednesday and desire the Lord's wisdom regarding treatment. Thanks everyone! "You will keep him in perfect peace, whose mind is stayed on You, because he trusts in You." Isaiah 26:2–4.

Chapter 2

The Tie that Binds

Some people, when they hear such frightening news, want to keep it to themselves and maybe share with immediate family and close friends. They are private people and certainly that is appropriate for them.

I am not like that. My life is an open book. I really appreciate the input and advice from others and certainly want to gather as much information as possible about whatever subject I am interested in at the time.

I began to search out for people who had had breast cancer, to explore their experiences, their reactions, their advice. I learned quickly that no two experiences are alike, no two sets of reactions the same, and I could not formulate a plan of attack or predict how I might react to the different situations I would be facing, based upon others' experiences.

It became abundantly clear that I would not be able to figure this out on my own—I needed the help of someone who already knew the end result. Only he could plan my days, and all I had to do was to rely on his knowledge. He does use others in my life to encourage me, to offer perspective; but the course I was on was mine alone, unique to me. That in itself was an encouragement.

Oh, I needed and wanted others to walk it with me, and it was imperative to do research to find out what the options were, but I could only count on Jesus to lead the way. He will place the people who I need in my path. He will give me the wisdom to know when to use the information that is shared and when to lean only upon the direction that he places within my heart.

It is incredible the peace that comes from that acceptance. I was certain, more than I think I had ever been before, of his love and support and that I could count on him to give me a sense of what steps to take and where to take them and the assurance to put one foot in front of the other without fear. Please don't misunderstand. I am not saying that it was easy or that I didn't get scared or that I didn't whine when it got tough or frustrated when it wasn't going the way I thought it should. Our emotions often will try to persuade us to go down the path of least resistance or follow a familiar road because it is more comfortable and less threatening to our sense of security, but this was a new path where there was no solace from things familiar. I must count upon the truth of his absolute and irrefutable love for me and that he would do what was needed just because I am his child.

And he did. I reached out and others reached out to me. I prayed, and people prayed for me. I sought out others, and others sought me out. I cried to him and he answered. I was supported by family, friends, people in my church, my pastor, coworkers, acquaintances, and healthcare providers. I received masses of cards and letters, emails, gifts, Facebook messages, and many calls of support. I was wrapped in the warmth of it all.

Each contact came at just the right time, a "rainbow" on a rainy day, an assurance of God's presence on a lonely night, and a smile when news was bitter. It was hard to comprehend sometimes that so many people cared. I have done nothing to deserve any of the kindnesses shown, but that is why they were so special—signs of unconditional love and acceptance. It leaves me awed and breathless—and thankful—and reminded me of his unconditional love.

God often meets our needs in unexpected ways. I had been concerned about how much time to take off for my surgery. The surgeon had said I should take a couple of weeks, but I knew that financially we could not afford that. I knew God could provide, but I have to admit I was concerned. I had no idea how much total time I would need through the entire period of treatment. I asked the surgeon how much recuperation time would be necessary, and he said I could go back to work as soon as I felt like I could, especially since I worked at home and could probably split my shift and work smaller blocks of time, but I was not to push myself beyond reasonable limits.

I called my supervisor and told her I was going to ask some of the other members of my team to see who might be willing to swap some time, so I could have a few days off together, and then, I would cover their shifts the few days before surgery. I was asked to hold off doing that until I heard back from her. Later on, in the afternoon, she called again and explained that the company wanted to provide me with the equivalent of two weeks paid time off, so I could have my surgery and recuperate appropriately without pushing to come back to work. *Wow.* All I could do was praise God for meeting that need. I am very blessed to work where I do, to be part of a work family that cares for one another, and where many of those in management also have a relationship with God.

On a snowy and cold day, on my way back from a chemo treatment, I received a card from an old friend I had not heard from in years. It wasn't just what was said in the note, but it meant so much that the person took the time to send it. It reminded me not to be complacent about doing the same for others. We really never know how God will use a word, a thought, a verse, a card, a call, or impromptu visit to minister to someone's heart.

Another need was met when our state's cancer society provided us with enough money to fill up our tank with heating oil, which was the equivalent of $600. I got a free wig from the American Cancer Society.

I must mention the hats! I love hats, and though going bald was okay and I didn't mind people seeing me that way, I loved wearing hats and now had a great reason to do so. Besides, I live in New England, and I was without hair during the fall and winter months, so going bald could get a bit chilly.

Once I had shaved my head, the hats started pouring in. I got hats from friends at my unhairy party, hats from coworkers who I had never met, and some I picked up at The Patrick Dempsey Center for Hope and Healing that were made by volunteers. People loved to see what hat I was going to wear next. I remember one Sunday at church when I was wearing a scarf, a little boy came up to me and told me I looked like a pirate.

Going to the mailbox became a very exciting part of my day. One day I might receive a check from someone who just wanted me to get something I needed or to put it toward medical bills. The next day would be a lovely card with a message of support. On still other days, I was blessed with a breast-cancer awareness Scentsy warmer, hats, a pretty shawl, a travel mug with pink ribbons, jewelry, a delivery of beautiful and big sunflowers accompanied by chocolate, and on it went. Each gift was lifting my spirits and yet humbling me that people would take their time and resources to show their support.

One of my favorite communications was from my husband, sent to me in eleven consecutive text messages:

To my wife: 10 Reasons to be Bald

1. No morning hair.
2. No bad hair days.
3. Can put the top down on the car.
4. No dandruff.
5. No helmet hair.
6. Don't have to buy shampoo.
7. Don't have to wait for conditioner to work in the shower.
8. Don't have to worry about going out with wet hair and catching a cold.
8. (yes, another 8—no one said I could count!) Don't have to worry about gray hair.
9. You can stand on your head and spin without worrying about having a bald spot.
10. Your husband will still love you just as much!

In writing this and reading through the various cards and notes received, I was reminded again of just how blessed I am. What a way to end a chapter and what a way to end a day.

> *"Pleasant words are like a honeycomb, sweetness to the soul and health to the bones."*
>
> *Proverbs 16:24*

Chapter 3

More Than Feelings

Throughout this recounting of my journey, I am going to share some mundane facts about my condition. I personally like to know details. Please know that though the narration of the specific diagnosis, treatment, and prognosis may seem devoid of feeling, processing those facts and statistics often aroused very strong emotions. The research and inquiries often validated the direction I was headed in making decisions about treatment. Conversely, they could also stir up concerns and fears about my future or about the pain or discomfort that I might have to endure.

I tried to deal with those concerns quickly, but sometimes I pushed them aside, not wanting to mess with them at that moment. Unchecked notions often drove my thoughts down rabbit trails with no real purpose except to confuse me, take my eyes off the one who had all the answers, and ultimately delay necessary decisions.

There was one night after surgery, I was trying to get comfortable in bed, having just diligently emptied my bulb drains and noted on a chart the amount of the drainage, situated my breast binder, carefully dressed for bed, all the time needing the help of one of my daughters to accomplish all these things. Finally, settling on a position that would work for the time being, I allowed all the frustration of feeling so helpless and the inability to move around like

I normally do to get to me. My thoughts went to dark places, one negative thought fueling another, and on and on it went until sleep was distant and the depths of despair were near.

I don't know how long this went on; I just know that I feasted on those thoughts until I was literally nauseous from the weight of it all. At some point in this despondency came the dawn of truth—that I needed to choose with my mind, over my emotions, to think about things that brought hope and moved me out of the dark places into the light, things like being alive, being able to share my experiences with others, able to learn more about myself through this process, this current situation would not last forever, and most of all, that the God of the universe was still very much in charge.

I placed considerable energy in focusing my mind on the truth of each scenario, so I would not react emotionally to exaggerated misconceptions of what might happen. We live in a world that has documented through story and film extraordinary and fantastic "realities" that have unfortunately desensitized us to what is actually true.

This matter-of-fact approach served me well. I wasn't always successful. Emotions are powerful things. Sometimes it felt "good" to react strongly, to wallow in self-pity, to get angry, or to just feel like throwing in the towel but only for a little while, because at some point, I would seek out a better emotional plane. I needed to move ahead as efficiently as possible. So, my goal was not to ignore those hard-to-contain thoughts and feelings but to put them in perspective and to place the feet of my mind on the solid ground of truth. I did not pretend or ignore that I was in pain or that I was feeling frustrated, but I chose to think about the probable temporariness of whatever was going on and that that circumstance did not have to bury me within it.

One Sunday, during the latter part of my radiation therapy, I was feeling very discouraged. It seemed that everything in my life was out of control because of this awful cancer. I was staying in a hospitality house, so I didn't have to travel back and forth in snow and ice. My dog was with my daughter. I could not plan anything that required much time, because I have to go to radiation therapy every weekday. I could not always work a full shift because of discomfort or fatigue. The amount that the insurance was not going to pay kept increasing, and I was starting to feel the physical side effects of the radiation.

The burns were causing pain that movement of my right arm exacerbated. I knew that I could stay home from church because of how I was feeling physically, but in my heart, I knew that I needed the encouragement and prayers of those in my church. I needed to worship the one who would get me through this situation and to get my eyes off my current condition. Many of my friends there knew that something was wrong when they saw me, asking me what the matter was. I told them the situation, knowing that they would pray.

Even though the pain was at the worst point it would be, I needed to think about the good that the treatment was doing—that I could continue doing what I needed to, working and taking care of my daily needs, and not succumb to the pain and frustration that could paralyze me from going forward both physically and emotionally.

I went back to the hospitality house and took a nap, got up and went to work, and before I knew it, I had put in my time and then some and realized the pain was nearly gone. I believe that it was my decision to focus on good things, God-directed thoughts, to busy my mind with other thoughts besides my dreary circumstances and the hope and reality that prayer would make a difference that resulted in that being the last day of having so much pain.

There was a time when the oncologist was sharing statistics with me. Okay, this means I could be the one out of four people who dies from this cancer. But wait, I could very well be one of the three out of four who survive. I'll go with visualizing that latter statistic for me because that is the one that will keep me hopeful and soaring ahead.

God created emotions, healthy emotions, to serve us, warn us, encourage us, and impassion us. We never should ignore emotions, but we should check those emotions to be sure they are reactions to the truth, God's truth, the reality, and not reactions to false or misunderstood information. If we are not careful, unchecked emotions will derail our progress, much like a broken road sign that has an arrow turning in the wrong direction.

It is clear that people often react best—or sometimes worst—to a person who is showing some feeling and engagement in what they are talking about. I believe God uses feelings in one person to connect with feelings in another. When I talked to a fellow breast-cancer survivor, it was their passion for being alive that assisted me in moving forward. It was their lack of despair that kept me away from dwelling in dark moments. Healthy emotions, both positive and negative, are needed to function appropriately, to minister to each other, to enjoy our surroundings, to be content in whatever situation we might find ourselves in, or to prompt us about potential danger or circumstances that will require our utmost attention. Being able to recognize the difference will help us to refocus on what is actually true and what is needed to take the next step.

I can think of an instance where I felt very sad and the tears ebbed and flowed. I am not sure what prompted the tears—probably I was thinking about all I was going through and feeling a bit apprehensive about what was to come. My future was uncertain after all. At first, I doubted my trust in God, thinking that the tears were a sign that I was frightened about what might happen to me, questioning that God had me in his sights.

I remember praying and asking God to speak to my heart about what was going on—and he did. In the quietness of the moment, he whispered that he saw no fear in my tears. One of the purposes for which he created them was to cleanse the human heart, to wash off the unnecessary debris, and to create fertile ground for him to work, so we can hear his voice more clearly. What a blessing to feel that kind of assurance through the simple act of crying. I am grateful that those tears drove me to the feet of the one who knew what I needed and to hear his voice encouraging me to keep moving forward.

That encouragement spurred me on to finish the journey, no matter how many detours, road blocks or pot holes there might be along the way.

> *"Hear, O Lord, when I cry with my voice! Have mercy also upon me, and answer me"*
>
> *(Psalms 27:7).*

Chapter 4

The Cancer Doc

Ever sit somewhere watching people? I think our reactions to what we see and what we imagine is going on in their lives are strongly affected by what is going on in our own. My daughter tells me I have a tendency to stare. I don't mean to be rude, but I get caught up in my imagination, wondering whether the young woman with the sad face is having conflict with her husband, or if the elderly lady walking very slowly has some medical condition that is making her life very difficult. Are they alone? Do they have someone who loves them enough to take care of them when they need it? Of course, we can never know what is happening in others' lives unless we ask, and that would be a very annoying thing to do. I am a nosy person, and so, I've been known to ask questions on occasion that others might think are intrusive.

After being diagnosed, I found that the context of my people-watching changed. Now, it seemed like I wondered if every person I saw either had cancer or their friend or loved one did.

When I was in the elevator going up to the second floor to see my oncologist for the first time, there were people with me who looked like nothing special was going on, that they were there doing something as natural as grocery shopping or a walk in the park. Did I look like that? Could they see the concern on my face, the anxiety about what I was going to hear in the next thirty minutes? After all, it had only been ten days since finding out I had breast cancer, and I was going to hear what would be happening over the next six months to a year of my life.

The moment finally arrived, one that I had anticipated greatly for over a week: meet my oncologist. He was a young man who was about to have his first child. Dr. Rausch was kind and straightforward. I perceived that he was feeling me out on just how blunt he could be, but I think he realized pretty quickly that he needed to just put it all out there. Within the first several visits, he mapped out my probable treatment course.

I was glad that we seemed to be a good "fit." It is very important for the well-being of a person with a serious illness to be comfortable with their healthcare providers: that how we see the treatment goals together is compatible and that we feel safe with the person who will be caring for us. Being able to work closely in establishing and working through the different aspects of treatment is critical. Gone are the days when you had to settle for whoever you had for a doctor, never questioning their decisions. Today, we are encouraged to get second and third opinions and to ask questions, do our own research, and make informed decisions with them about our care. We have a choice about what our treatment will look like, and the final decision is really ours.

According to the initial needle biopsy done after my mammogram, the preliminary diagnosis was invasive ductal carcinoma (IDC). This is the most common type of breast cancer, found in eighty percent of the cases. There was a possibility that it could also be invasive medullary carcinoma, a rare subtype of IDC, making up about three to five percent of all cases. It is called "medullary" carcinoma because the tumor is a soft, fleshy mass that resembles a part of the brain called the medulla.

Later on, final pathology from surgery would determine that the cancer was indeed medullary carcinoma. At first, it was felt that the tumors were stage 1 because they were relatively small.

"Stage" is based on four different characteristics of the tumor: size, invasive or noninvasive, whether it is found in lymph nodes, and whether it has spread to other parts of the body. This would be determined definitively at the time of surgery.

The grade of the tumor on the initial needle biopsy was two in one mass and three in the other. "Grade" is a score that tells you how different the cancer cells' appearance and growth patterns are from those of normal, healthy cells. Grade 2 cancer cells do not look like normal cells and grow and divide a little faster than normal. Grade 3 cells look very different from normal cells. They grow quickly in disorganized, irregular patterns, with many dividing to make new cancer cells.

After having surgery, we discussed chemotherapy treatment in more detail based on the results of the final pathology, which bumped the stage up to 2A. They combined the sizes of the two masses and the fact that I had one positive lymph node to determine this stage. It was determined to be grade 3 in both masses. They could not determine if I had two distinct masses or whether one mass had spread into the surrounding tissue resulting in the second mass.

It was recommended that I have dose-dense chemotherapy—every two weeks instead of the normal every-three-week schedule—of doxorubicin, cyclophosphamide, and paclitaxel. Doxorubicin and cyclophosphamide would be given together every two weeks for four treatments and then the paclitaxel alone every two weeks for four treatments for a total of eight treatments over sixteen weeks.

The total length of the chemotherapy sessions could range from two to four hours depending on the drugs involved and the infusion rate. Some drugs should be infused more slowly, so the body does not react as strongly to its administration.

He explained the definite and possible side effects, like, hair loss (definitely), nausea (likely), and possibly low blood count, diarrhea, rash, vomiting, and peripheral neuropathy (tingling and numbness in fingers and toes), and some less likely occurrences, such as, bone pain, heart damage, as well as others. I would need to take steroids and a dietary supplement (L-glutamine) with the paclitaxel to hopefully reduce the severity of the peripheral neuropathy that I would most probably get as well as a rare condition that could result in my capillaries (small blood vessels) leaking blood.

Since one of the side effects to one of the drugs is heart damage, I would need to have a MUGA scan of my heart to make sure there was no preexisting heart disease. I would also need to take Neulasta shots to assist with making new white blood cells if my blood count went too low.

The treatment course was charted: A surgery would be needed to remove the tumors and probably the entire breast and then a port placement is done so that they would not have to do an IV for each chemo session. Chemotherapy and radiation therapy would probably be necessary and then definitely hormonal therapy would be done for at least five years. Some tumors can grow with the help of certain hormones, like, estrogen and progesterone. Hormonal therapy decreases the amounts of certain hormones that the body releases. My cancer was positive for the estrogen receptor, so I would need the hormonal suppression treatment.

He also shared with me the statistics based on my age (fifty-seven years old), general health (fair), estrogen receptor status (positive), tumor size (two masses combined were in the 2.1 to 3.0 cm range), nodes involved (one out of three), and the type of chemotherapy. Ten-year survival percentage was presented based on four different decision scenarios:

1. No additional therapy: Fifty percent of women are alive in ten years; forty-three percent of women die because of cancer; seven percent of women die from other causes.
2. Hormonal therapy alone: Sixty-one percent of women are alive in ten years, a gain of eleven percent due to just hormonal therapy.
3. Chemotherapy alone: Sixty-six percent of women are alive in ten years; an additional sixteen percent are alive due to chemotherapy alone.
4. Combined therapy: Seventy-three percent of women are alive in ten years; an additional twenty-three percent are alive due to combined therapy.

As one can see, combined treatment improves the likelihood of survival at the ten-year mark. Of course, none of us can know when our time will come, but I wanted the best chance of surviving this cancer and chose the combined therapy. I do not want to be the one out of four who does not live to see my grandchildren get married or have great-grandchildren. I want to live to see retirement and to enjoy many years with my family. I want to live in the Southwest again. I want to die the natural death of old age.

On my elevator ride back down from that first visit with my oncologist, I wondered if the people who rode with me knew that my life had irrevocably changed, at least my physical life. You see, I know that who I am inside will be the same, perhaps rough edges softened and smoothened like clay in a potter's hand and then refined by the fire of tough circumstances. Of course, they could not see into my life any more than I could see into theirs, but there was one who knew and there were those around me who saw and who cared and who loved, and that was okay—that was more than okay.

> *"Have I not commanded you? Be strong and of good courage; do not be afraid, nor be dismayed, for the Lord your God is with you wherever you go"*
> *(Joshua 1:9).*

08.25.11—Oncologist visit today. See the surgeon next week. Then once final pathology back, will decide on best course of treatment. Your prayers continue to be appreciated. Thanks for the support you've shown; it means so much! God's grace is sufficient.

08.25.11—Email: I do not have a lot of information just yet. But here is the scoop as of the moment. For some of you this may be the first time you have heard of my situation, but I felt it was time to get you into the loop. The process only started about two weeks ago. If you desire not to be kept updated, I understand, and just let me know.

Cancer type: Invasive ductal carcinoma, grade three in one mass and grade two in the other (both in one breast). This is the most common type of breast cancer (80%). Differential is invasive medullary carcinoma. They cannot tell by the needle biopsy if these are two distinct masses or if one mass has already spread from the other.

I see the surgeon next Wednesday. We will then decide if I will have a lumpectomy/partial mastectomy with radiation therapy or a mastectomy. At this point, I feel that I would want a mastectomy as I do not want radiation unless absolutely necessary. If recommended and a reasonable option, I may have both breasts removed if it increases the likelihood that cancer will not return.

The surgery will then also include either sentinel node biopsy or lymph node dissection. Once the final pathology is back, they will then have a multidisciplinary tumor conference to recommend the treatment course. I will have to have healed from surgery before chemotherapy can begin, if that is recommended.

Since I was ER (estrogen receptor) positive (but PR negative and HER2 negative), I will definitely be on hormonal treatment for five years, probably with an aromatase inhibitor, like Arimidex. After five years, they will reassess whether hormonal treatment needs to continue.

Interestingly, if chemotherapy is recommended, they may seek insurance approval for the OncotypeDX test (approximately $4000) to determine my likely response to chemotherapy. However, the doctor says sometimes the test comes back equivocal and doesn't help much in treatment decisions, but sometimes it is very helpful.

As far as how I am doing: Well, not my great peace and I implicitly trust him with my future. However, sometimes my emotions run away with me and I begin to worry about what the future holds. God is gracious and understands those emotions, but is quick to remind me that his grace is sufficient,

That's the update for now...more news to come next week!

Again your thoughts and prayers mean a lot. If you attend church and they have a prayer chain that does not already list this prayer request, please consider adding at your discretion.

P.S. I am blessed to have many resources here with a local cancer center and The Patrick Dempsey Center for Cancer Hope & Healing (McDreamy from Gray's Anatomy, who grew up in Maine). They have great resources and education available.

Chapter 5

Preparing for Change

My husband gave me the nickname "Boobie" early on in our relationship. The reason was pretty clear. I was certainly not flat-chested, and admittedly, he was a man who was attracted most to that part of a woman. He even stenciled this endearment on the passenger side of the clunker he used to go back and forth to work. It was an impulsive act he later regretted when I refused to ride with him anymore. Eventually, after a few embarrassing situations with that particular pet name, one of which was a yell across a church sanctuary after a service, he shortened it to Boo. I am forever grateful.

I had done a lot of research about mastectomy and the reasons why it was recommended. There were a lot of blogs and posts that discussed women's heart-rending confessions about how difficult it was to lose, what was for some, the essence of who they thought they were. I realized that who I was as a person was not based on my physical attributes but who I was in my spirit and in my heart and ultimately based on who Jesus says I am.

In a very pragmatic decision, I was willing to have my breast removed because there was a medical reason to do so. I knew I would have an emotional response to the loss once it actually happened. Not that I would not do it, but I knew I would have to deal with those deep feelings connected to my womanhood once that part of me was gone. I had also determined that if there was any increased survival rate by having both breasts removed, I would do that. I figured it would be less traumatic for me to be no-chested rather than lop-chested.

I had to talk to my husband. After all, breasts are an important part of attraction, of lovemaking, and of physical beauty. There was a reason he had nicknamed me Boobie; I needed to know how he really felt about this probability.

I have kiddingly (well, I think I was kidding) called my husband a pure redneck. He grew up in a family who worked in the woods and ran a sawmill. All the kids in the family worked with the adults from the time they were old enough to do so until they left home. He thought like a man; he was quite independent and sometimes quite stubborn. But, he was a knight in shining armor for me and my children.

Having been in a physically and emotionally abusive relationship prior to this, his no-nonsense attitude and kindness was a life raft for us. It took us some time to heal from those damaged psyches and learn to trust again, but it happened. Even though many people thought Keith and I were an odd couple, we worked. We argued well and loved well. It was clear that I would never have to worry about being physically hurt again. It just wasn't in his nature.

One day, as we sat watching television, I asked him if we could talk. I told him the information I had garnered about mastectomy and that it may be—probably would be—necessary for me. "What do you think about that?" I asked.

As was true to my husband's nature, his response was predictable, "It is your decision, and I'll support whatever you decide."

Okay, we need to move down deeper in this conversation. After some prodding on my part, we came to the crux of the discussion. I think he realized he could not just abdicate responsibility for this decision because it affected him too in a very real way. We discussed whether he felt that reconstruction was important to him; it was not important to me. He stated it was not. In my heart, I knew he would rather I be a flat-chested alive woman, than a large-breasted sick one.

Fortunately, Keith was able to be home, and my daughter Cassie was able to go the day we first visited with Dr. D'Augustine, the surgeon at the Bennett Breast Care Center. I found it very helpful to have someone go to all my appointments with me. They helped me remember the discussions and information, which sometimes seemed overwhelming.

Initially, the doctor wanted to ultrasound my right axilla, on the side where the cancer was, to see if he could tell whether any lymph nodes looked worrisome, which they did not to his eye.

He explained that the tumor board would meet to discuss my case. Tumor boards are a conference where cancer specialists discuss patients. Generally, these conferences include surgeons, medical oncologists, radiation oncologists, pathologists, radiologists, and other cancer specialists. In most cases, the tumor board will reach a consensus for a treatment plan for each patient presented. In my case, they were recommending mastectomy, chemotherapy, radiation therapy, and hormonal therapy. The specifics of the treatment would be decided once final pathology came back from surgery.

The surgery would be a modified radical mastectomy with a sentinel lymph-node biopsy and removal of lymph nodes, if needed. Since I was not interested in reconstruction, that would not be performed and would decrease surgery and recuperation time. A modified radical mastectomy without reconstruction takes two to four hours and usually involves a one-night hospital stay. A single incision across half the chest usually allows the surgeon to remove the breast and lymph nodes, if needed.

After the mastectomy, a small tube is placed in the breast area to draw off fluid. The end of this drain is attached to a pocket-sized suction device. The drainage would be monitored, and the device would be removed once the drainage was minimal. The purpose of the drain is to remove excessive fluid that accumulates after surgery. If the fluid is not drained, a seroma, a pocket of fluid, can develop, which can be painful and may become infected.

I asked Dr. D'Augustine if having both breasts removed would increase my survival rate. He stated by perhaps five percent. He did say it was my decision, and so I asked him to remove both.

The surgeon was a kind-looking upper middle-aged gentleman who reminded me of Groucho Marx. I instantly felt at ease. He stated that I had a "great chance of beating this." Although I knew that "chance" was not what I had on my side, as there are no chances with God, I appreciated his encouragement.

There have been great advances in the treatment of cancer and especially of breast cancer. The reality is, however, there are those whose cancer grows and spreads quickly and for whom treatment is futile. I hope I am not one of those people; but if I am, that will just be another journey that I will embark upon. For now, I will focus on the current trek and take the next step to surgery.

> *"But as it is written, 'Eye has not seen, nor ear heard, nor have entered into the heart of man the things which God has prepared for those who love Him"*
> *(1 Corinthians 2:9).*

Social Media Posts and Emails

08.31.11—Email: IDC (invasive ductal carcinoma), clinical stage I—great news! What an answer to prayer! This could change once looked at microscopically after removed at time of surgery.

Surgery for bilateral mastectomies and sentinel lymph node biopsy on Thursday, September 15, in the a.m. Overnight stay in the hospital at Central Maine Medical Center. Three to four days' recovery time at home. The surgeon's words: "You have a great chance of beating this." But, we knew that all along as there is no "chance" when it is the Lord making the decisions.

Then within a month after surgery, they will make recommendations for future treatment, that is, hormone therapy (a pill every day for five years), chemotherapy, and radiation therapy (one or a combination of all/any of these 3).

God is so good. He has exchanged any anxiousness on my part with his perfect peace. He has assured me of his steadfast love and that he will never leave me alone. Each day is easier than the day before because I know my future is safe with him—whatever it might look like. Besides drawing me closer to you, Lord, what are you going to teach me during this time??

Thanks again for all your prayers and support. I really appreciate it.

09.01.11—Stage I (yeah! definite answer to prayer) invasive ductal carcinoma. Surgery in two weeks. Then on to treatment once pathology is back. God is good!

09.01.11—Email: I just got a call from my supervisor, and my employer has decided to give me a gift of $1000 so that I can take off the needed time to recover from my surgery. They did not want me worrying about work and schedules and switching with people, etc. They just want me to take care of myself and get better. God is so good and what a wonderful blessing.

09.11.11—Email: Hi everyone,

Your thoughts and prayers have been such an encouragement and definitely have been felt. I don't understand how prayer works—but I know it does. I have felt comforted and at peace, and I know for sure that it has to do with the amount of people praying and sending their thoughts and encouragements.

This week marks twenty-six days since I found out I have invasive ductal carcinoma, a malignant tumor of my right breast with two different masses. As you can imagine, at first I was filled with fear of the unknown, what will I have to go through, how sick will I get, will they have to do surgery, is radiation in my future, will I be taking that five-year prescription pill, and on and on. But with each passing day, Jesus has assured me he is taking this trip with me and we will truly face it together. I see him in the many people who pray, speak, care, laugh, cry, encourage, educate, and yell at me.

Talking with others that have had different forms and even the same type of cancer was helpful, but the truth is there are no two people alike and no two people are treated the same. This is an individual journey, but it certainly is not one I have to take alone.

Foremost, I have a God who loves me and will never leave me—no matter how grouchy I get in the process or when sometimes I think he has left. His presence is so near that I know I can count on it as much as I can count on anything that I can touch. My little tumors do not separate me from his love—in fact, in one sense they are an answer to a prayer for a closer walk with him. This condition has been a part of my future for my whole life and is not a surprise to him—just to me. I know that God never wastes a wound and that he will use this circumstance to his glory. Perhaps I can be an encouragement to someone else.

Secondly, my family has been so supportive. Keith has cried with me, laughed with me (making some jokes at my expense, I dare say), and has conveyed his unwavering support. (I will have to remind him of that during those "honey, can I have…or will you help…?" for the umpteenth time. Luv, I love you with all my heart.

Thirdly, my children. Each in their own way has laughed and cried with me, assuring me of help whenever and wherever I need it (oh, boy, you better watch out…). I love them dearly because I can see that right now they are thinking of me more than themselves.

I can't forget my friends. You have written me notes, called me on the phone, lifted me up in your thoughts and prayers, and have encouraged me. I can't imagine going through this without your help. There is no way to let you know the tears of joy that I have had just from reading a small note in the mailbox, or a word of encouragement on Facebook, or a special email with caring words, or the phone calls that choke me up to think that there really are people who care enough to share of themselves. (This has happened with family, too, but I consider my friends my family too.)

This week will bring its own challenges and hurdles, but my eyes are on the prize! Do I know what the prize is yet? No, but boy I know it is going to be good. Thursday morning I will be having the bilateral mastectomies (no reconstruction). They say as long as things go well I will probably be home on Friday. Keith will be staying at home with me until Sunday evening, at which time one of my daughters will come and stay with me for a few days. Hopefully I will be back to myself, a little lighter than I was before (what a way to lose weight...) The good thing is they both know how to cook.

I will miss my first Monday Bible study, but hopefully no more than that. I will miss Sunday church but am hoping to have a video. Wal-Mart won't see me for a few days (I can hear it groaning...) Work knows I may be up to two weeks before coming back. Oh and my work, what a blessing they have been with team members and management letting me know they are there, thinking about me, encouraging me not to worry about work, and for those who are Christians putting me on their prayer chains at church. Some have told me their stories of surviving cancer. There was even a surprise from the company that will make it easier to rest during my recuperation.

The bottom line to this lengthy email is this: Life often doesn't go the way we plan or even think, but when it takes that detour, we can know that there is someone who cares and wants to take the journey with us as long as we let them (God, friends, family, co-workers, other survivors).

I will update everyone after the surgery. Lots of love coming your way…

From my cancer journal, Tuesday, 09.13.11: The peace of God is a KNOWING and not a feeling. Knowing that You always have my best interest and Your kingdom at the core of every situation. My prayer is that this time will not be wasted on self-pity, fears and doubts, but it will be a time of resting in Your complete and utter love for me.

To my family and friends on FB: Your continued prayers as I continue on my breast cancer journey: This week bilateral mastectomies on Thursday. Please pray for the procedure and those involved, for my family as they help to care for me, and for me as I get used to losing something I have had for so long. Prayer has made such a difference; I have felt it and I have great peace. God is awesome and is teaching me more about himself during this time—what more could I ask…

09.14.11—From the Breast Cancer Site: When breast cancer is found early, the five-year survival rate is 96%. From me: Yeah! Praise the Lord!

Chapter 6

Scalpels Away

September 15, 2011

It had been one month to the day since hearing the news. A lot had happened over those four weeks. My daughter Heather had to have a surgery to remove her gallbladder. I had visited with the oncologist on my daughter Cassie's birthday. I had cried, I had laughed, I had ruminated, I had prayed, I had discussed, I had shared, I had listened, I had read and re-read, I had researched, and I had decided.

Through it all, I knew the peace of God that really did pass all understanding. Each day and each step was one taken in total trust in the one who had my back. I had people who loved me and would be there for me. I had a heavenly father who didn't mind that I sometimes needed to crawl up into his lap and just weep or hold on tight. But then, after that sweet time of intimate fellowship and comfort, I would be ready to climb down and go about the business of living.

The surgery date had been set and the day had come. I should have no food after midnight and should be up at 3:45 a.m. to shower with some special soap. Both Heather and Cassie had spent the night at my house, and Keith had gotten home in the wee hours of the morning. We headed to the hospital for arrival at 5:30 a.m. The day had finally come. I would be a different person when I saw my home again, at least physically.

I had my pretty pink footies with the breast-cancer ribbon that my friend Angie had given to me. The nurses had me change into the dreaded backless gown and protective cap. I put on my familiar footies, but to my dismay, they would not let me wear them to surgery; I had to wear the dull gray hospital ones. Ho-hum.

My wearing those pink slippers was not a big deal, but what they symbolized was. I was now one of the elite people suffering from breast cancer, the one in eight, and I wanted to wrap myself in the support and love that those little pink footies represented. However, there was no time to weep over seemingly small things, when I was facing major surgery that would change me forever. Having answered questions and been poked numerous times to establish an IV, I am now ready.

Pastor Tim arrived, and he and Keith came in to pray with me before they took me to radiology. I don't know why their presence was so emotional for me. I think I had kept my nervousness and fragile emotions in check up until that point. My pastor's willingness to come to the hospital so early in the morning to pray for me was moving; it opened up the flood gates, and I just couldn't stop the tears from coming. He prayed for God's presence to be real and for God's protection over the surgery. I had not known Pastor Tim long, but it was clear that he had a pastor's heart and had been faithful in encouraging me and checking on me.

I was then whisked down to the radiology department where I got the radioactive material injected for the sentinel lymph-node biopsy. A sentinel node is the first lymph node to which cancer cells are most likely to spread from a primary tumor. A sentinel lymph-node biopsy is the procedure where the sentinel node is identified, removed, and examined to see if cancer cells are present. In order to find this node, they need to inject radioactive material into the area of the tumor. After a period of time, the surgeon uses a device that can detect the radioactivity to find the sentinel node. That node is removed and examined by a pathologist. If cancer is present, other nodes may be removed and examined as well.

The technician explains that he will inject the radioactive material in an area on the outside of the nipple area. Well that sounds like fun. He says that the discomfort varies in intensity but usually feels like a bee sting. Well, I have been stung by a bee, so this shouldn't be so bad. I lie on the table and the tech injects the material. If I were a swearing person, I am sure that the halls of the CMMC Radiology Department would have reverberated with unseemly vulgarity that would have made even my mother blush (you had to have known my mother to appreciate this reference).

Bee sting, yeah right, if the bee is the size of a helicopter!

"Take a deep breath and rub," he tells me. Massaging the area promotes the spread of the material to the lymph nodes. I remind myself it will be over soon. I am not going to focus on what just happened; I am going to think about what heaven is going to be like… where there is no pain and no helicopter-sized bees.

The pain didn't last long, but it is not a procedure that I would ever want to go through again. Oh wait, that's right, I won't have to.

I am wheeled back to my presurgery room where I have just a few minutes to visit with my family before I am taken to the operating suite.

In the preop area, I meet with the anesthesiologist. I let her know that on one occasion in the past, I came out of a surgery with what felt like an elephant on my chest and that after the most recent two surgeries, I had felt really anxious in the postop area when they were trying to wake me up, feeling stuck between sleeping and wakefulness and the fear that I couldn't wake up. I would hear the nurses calling my name, and I couldn't answer them. It was really a terrifying feeling.

She seemed optimistic that they could help with that. And they did. I do not remember a thing in the immediate postoperative time. The first thing I remember is being wheeled back to my room. Thank you, Lord.

My family was waiting for me. After the nurses got me situated and placed me in a pretty pink flowered breast binder that would help with discomfort and hopefully prevent the formation of hematomas and/or seromas (localized collection of blood or other fluid), I was able to visit.

I felt tired but happy it was over. At one point, I looked down and the familiar hills were gone and in their place were small valleys. Again, the tears just came. I was not ashamed of my reaction and didn't try to stop it. Sometimes, we just need to grieve for a bit and then it is easier to move on.

Fortunately, there was very little incisional pain. As is usually the case, the nerve areas are also cut in a mastectomy, so the only real soreness was where the drains entered the body. They had been stitched in place, so they could not be accidentally pulled out. I could only lie on my back, because there was some general discomfort when lying on my side. Having no postoperative complications, I was released the next day.

I was happy to be back home. And yes, I looked different than when I left, but then there are many times in our lives when just a few days, a few hours, or a few minutes can change things for us. We can either go down into the deep place of despair or we can take the next step, knowing we have people walking next to us who will make each step a little easier and a friend who is always there.

The girls took turns staying with me once Keith went back to work. I had to have help to put the binder on, to get in and out of bed, and in and out of a chair. Making a meal was clumsy and often difficult because these necessary drain appendages were smacked dab in the middle of my frontside. I slept a lot for a few days, not always a restful sleep, but one interrupted by crazy, convoluted dreams or waking up every so often, because I couldn't get comfortable. Surgery is an assault on the body, and no matter the extent, the body needs to use vital resources that leave us feeling tired and weak.

The drains were doing their job, but one of them was still putting out quite of bit of fluid, and I had the drain in a week longer than is usual. They were bulky and in the way, often getting caught or pulled inadvertently. My sixty-pound dog, Lexie, did not understand that she couldn't jump up on me for her normal loving, and I feared she would misunderstand my pushes to get down as me rejecting her.

I was allergic to the antibiotic that was being used around the irritated drain sites. A change in antibiotic cream cleared that problem.

Finally, the surgeon decided that he was going to remove the last drain anyway as there was a risk of infection the longer it stayed in. It felt so good to have them gone. They were necessary but such a bother. Their presence made it look like my breasts had shriveled up and taken residence about four inches below where they originally were.

When so much is going awry in our lives, we need to take the great moments and allow them to lift our spirits, to give us the hope that there will be more moments that will encourage us and put smiles on our faces, even though sometimes they are only Mona Lisa smiles.

On the follow-up visit to the surgeon, we were informed that one of the lymph nodes was positive for metastatic cancer. The other two were not cancerous. He said this might change the chemotherapy regimen, but he did not feel that any more lymph nodes needed to be removed. I was relieved as removing more axillary lymph nodes can result in lymphedema, a condition which causes the arm to swell, sometimes permanently. Otherwise I was doing well and was cleared to proceed to the next waypoint, which was the port placement and then chemotherapy.

> *"God, you are so faithful. I know you are with each microstep I am taking. I feel your presence, sometimes more than others, but I know you are there whether I feel your presence or not. Now, Lord, the next big steps are coming, another milestone on my journey. Show me the way; keep me balanced and oriented. My biggest fear right now is that I will not always appreciate all you have done for me—that in those moments when I feel so sick, or hurt so much, or am so tired I cannot even sleep and that I won't remember all the good things that you have done for me. When my mind is confused from physical*

ailments, remind me so I can remind others of your absolute faithfulness."

"You will keep him in perfect peace, whose mind is stayed on You, because he trusts in You"

(Isaiah 26:3).

Social Media Posts and Emails

Wakefield cancer journal, 09.17.11: Lord, I may be sore and weigh a little less, but I am still your child uniquely and wonderfully made. I pray God's blessing on all those who prayed and are praying. Very little pain, do not remember waking up from anesthesia (that is a good thing) and now at home where my hunny is waiting on me—except when he tells me I should get up and move around a bit...Luv to all.

Wakefield Cancer Update 09.21.11. Postop visit with surgeon today. Mastectomy incisions look good, drains must remain for a few more days at least (ugh). Stage has been bumped up to stage 2 because of one of three positive sentinel lymph nodes. Type of cancer has changed to invasive medullary carcinoma (a rarer type but not treated any differently). Visit with radiation oncology (possible radiation therapy to armpit versus additional surgery to remove. First, I want to thank all those who have called, sent cards/gifts, cooked food, and/or visited. These caring demonstrations of your care and concern mean more to me than you can imagine right now. As I have said before, the peace of God has been overwhelming at times; and during those moments where the emotions surface, I allow them to do their job (since God gave them to me for a reason) and then refocus on his love, care and perfect plan for me.

Secondly, I visited with the surgeon today. The multidisciplinary team met this morning before my appointment. The final pathology report changed in that the type of cancer is different than originally thought. It is now considered an invasive medullary carcinoma (a rarer type). It had spread to one of the three sentinel lymph nodes, so this bumped the staging up to a stage II. However, there are a couple of options regarding the rest of the lymph nodes in the axilla, which are either surgery to remove them or radiation therapy to the armpit. I have a consultation with the radiation oncologist on Monday. After that consultation, we will make a decision on whether to have additional surgery to remove more lymph nodes to check them for metastatic cancer or to have focused radiation to that area—I have been assured that the jury is out on which may have the better prognosis. However, surgery has complications like infection and lymphedema, neither of which sound appealing in that I need to use that arm for work. The surgeon is still very optimistic about a good prognosis.

I have an appointment with the oncologist on Friday next week and then we will (hopefully) make decisions about whether we will proceed with chemotherapy. The surgeon said "If it were me, I would go with radiation therapy to the armpit and chemotherapy."

I believe that God had already begun to ready my heart for this eventuality in that I was not surprised nor upset about the news. (I dreamt the other night I saw the radiation oncologist.) God has known from the beginning of time what my course and prognosis are, and I am very content in knowing that.

I would ask prayer for a confirmation in my spirit when given choices about what road to take and that the resources needed (rides, finances, etc.) will be available for whatever is decided upon. Everyone has been so gracious and offering assistance and should radiation therapy be needed, I may very well need assistance with rides to and from (as it is usually daily for a few weeks).

May God bless you today and bring you a sense of peace of his awesome power, love, and purpose.

Cancer Journal 09.22.11: Lord, you see the tears, but I really do trust you. "Child, I know there is no real fear in your tears. I have given them to you to cleanse your heart and mind of unnecessary fears and to wash my Truth over them."

From Heather on 09.25.11: To my mother, my fighter, my hero:

Though it is early in the diagnosis,
I will fight with you every day.
Though it will be a rough road ahead,
I will fight with you every day.
While some days will feel like you just can't go on,
I will fight with you every day.
For you have been the one constant in my life,
Who has fought with me every day.
You have been my strength when I thought I had none,
A shoulder when I needed to cry,
My sounding board when I needed to vent,
My rock when I've needed an anchor.
I want you to know you are not alone.
I will be here,
To be your strength when you have none.
Your shoulder when you need to cry.
Your sounding board when you need to vent.
Your rock when you need an anchor.
You are my hero, my fighter, and most importantly, my mom.
I love you!

Chapter 7

A Port in the Storm

Ever since I can remember, I have had trouble with being stuck to draw blood. My veins are small and hard to find. I have had needle sticks in the upper arm, lower arm, hand, and almost in the big toe because they couldn't find a viable vein anywhere else. When I found out I was going to have chemotherapy, one of my primary concerns was about the feasibility of having an IV placed each time. IVs usually cause painful bruising and often infiltrate the surrounding tissues because my veins don't stand up well to the assault.

Routinely, a port is placed by a surgeon to provide a safe and relatively easy way to administer the chemotherapy, but it is also used to draw blood to check cell counts, which they do prior to giving the chemo to make sure that red and white blood cells are in the right range to receive it. The port itself is a reservoir that is attached to a long catheter. The type of port I had inserted was a PowerPort, which is triangular in shape and had three "bumps" at each point that are used to palpate it under the skin, so they know where to put the access needle.

I was told that this was a day procedure and so did not anticipate any issues, although the surgeon warned me that sometimes they have a hard time finding the internal jugular vein on "fluffy" ladies like me. Little did I know that this seemingly small part of my treatment journey was going to be anything but…

On arrival at the hospital, we went to the minor surgery center, sometimes called ambulatory surgery or day surgery, and checked in. Keith and Cassie accompanied me, and we waited patiently. When they were ready for me, I was given the familiar hospital gown and cap to change into and was settled onto a gurney.

We went through all the necessary questions and paperwork. They established an IV for the sedation that I would receive and took my vital signs (temperature, blood pressure, heart rate, respiratory rate, and oxygen saturation). They gave me oodles of information, and it seemed like they told me everything I could expect. Keith and Cassie sat with me while I waited for the surgeon. We talked and joked.

Fortunately, there were no machines in the room that would tempt my husband to check how they worked nor did I see disposable Latex gloves anywhere around that would provide comic relief for him. He has been known to push buttons to find out what a machine will do, once causing an automatic blood pressure cuff to practically explode in its holster while pushing every button in sight to try to stop its expansion. A Latex glove really got his juices flowing; he would draw funny faces on a blown-up glove and then watch the face shrivel as he indiscreetly lets the air out. He has been frowned upon by many healthcare workers as I sit by and try to deny knowing him.

I was relaxed and ready to go when I was told my surgeon had arrived. I was wheeled down to the procedure area. It was a relatively small room, not as big as the usual operating room. There was a fluoroscopy machine and other necessary equipment. Fluoroscopy is a study of moving body structures; think of it as an X-ray "movie."

A continuous X-ray beam is passed through the part of the body being examined and transmitted to a monitor, so the body part and inserted device and its motion can be seen in detail. The surgeon makes a small incision in the upper chest, just below the clavicle, feeds the catheter into the internal jugular vein, and places the port device just under the skin. By using fluoroscopy, the surgeon can make sure that the catheter is placed correctly in the correct vein without having to do a more invasive procedure to directly see and feel that it is in the right place. Once placed, the incision is closed over it.

Surprisingly, it seemed to me that there were a lot of people in this room for such a routine and minor procedure. Now, I believe in education, and I don't mind participating in teaching moments, even when I am the patient. However, my gown is quickly turned down in order to prepare my chest. Well, I have had surgery and my breasts are gone; now in their place are two horizontal incisions that are in the final stages of healing. There are at least three people standing around the fluoroscopy unit which is about three feet away, two of whom were men, and probably two to three others who were circulating around the room, preparing it and me for the procedure.

I mean, *"Really? do you need three people to run the fluoroscopy? Do you need to be here while my chest is unceremoniously uncovered and prepared?"* It hit me hard. I am in this vulnerable position, my front side laid wide open for everyone to see, with long ugly horizontal scars where my breasts used to be. I know they have seen it before and mean me no disrespect. My hope is that I won't become fodder for later conversation or jokes.

It is easier for me to process events if you give me advance notice of what to expect. That way, I can prepare myself. No one told me how many people were going to be in these tight quarters with me, and it was really disconcerting that there were five to six people in this room already and the surgeon had not even arrived yet. I was finding it hard to talk because I was afraid that if I opened my mouth, I would start to cry, and then, I would be even more embarrassed. So, I lay there, trying to keep my mind on something positive, hoping it would end quickly, while all these people were milling about me, seemingly unaware of anything I was going through.

Though I remain silent, my mind is yelling: *"Hey, remember me, I'm the patient. I'm the one you are here to take care of. Don't forget I am a person with feelings. Don't you know this is hard for me?"*

The surgeon came to the door, which was partially open this whole time, with a pretty young lady. He informed me that she is an intern working with him that day and did I mind if she observed.

My mouth said it is fine, but my heart was having its own dialogue: *"Well sure...why not...what's another set of eyes on my deformed body. Did you really expect me to say 'no' with her standing there and when obviously there were already an inordinate number of people watching? Why didn't you have the staff ask me that question when I was getting ready?"*

As you can understand, I wasn't in the best frame of mind. My mother would have said, "Sure! The more, the merrier!" and meant it. Me, I just laid in morbid embarrassment wishing it was over and I was on my way home.

I think healthcare workers sometimes forget that the people they are serving may have mixed feelings about the procedures and processes they are undergoing. It is such a common occurrence to them that they don't always think about how the patient may be feeling and empathize in a way that validates those feelings and avoids unnecessary embarrassment. It was my perception they were oblivious that I might be embarrassed or upset. Fortunately, it was a short time before I was being sedated and had no idea at that point what was happening to me or who was there. Thank heaven for anesthesia!

After being brought out of the sedation, they took me back to the preprocedural area and waited for me to fully wake up, gave me discharge instructions, and sent me on my way. But I couldn't shake how upset I was about the process. I kept picturing myself lying there, exposed, with all these people's eyes on me. I chose not to speak up at the time because I am one that has to think through what I am going to say, so I can rationally give an appropriate response. I certainly did not want to unload on people who were doing their job, even if I felt that a better explanation about what to expect just prior to the procedure should have been given.

It was a very humbling experience. I asked the Lord to take away my sense of violation and replace it with his peace, which he ultimately did. However, he chose not to immediately remove all the emotions surrounding the event for a reason, probably not the least of which was so that I would follow up and make suggestions for future patients.

It would take me almost six months before I told anyone about what happened, and it still brought tears to my eyes as I recounted it. I was glad, though, that someone within the facility finally asked about my experiences, both positive and negative. They were very positive except for this one event. I hope they will consider preparing patients better, even for minor procedures, when the nature of the procedure means that the person will have intimate body areas exposed for all the world to see, well at least the "world" that is in the room.

As I discussed again with my husband what had happened on that day, I believe that the Lord gave me some insight into my state of mind at the time. All humans are control freaks, and yes, I am human. We want to control our environment and our circumstances so that what happens is comfortable and predictable. When one is diagnosed with a devastating illness like cancer, we quickly realize that many things are now out of our control. Oh, I know that God is ultimately in charge, because I have asked him to be, and I trust him with my life, but he allows us to take some ownership in our actions.

We are not his puppets, and he has given us free will. Too often, we want to maneuver and manipulate what is going on around us just so we don't feel lost, alone, unbalanced. Ultimately, if he is Lord in our lives, we realize that it is okay not to be in control, that things happen as they do for a reason, and that all our experiences, whether positive, negative, or inconsequential, are just different mediums and colors that God is using to paint our ultimate picture—his masterpiece, which will speak in our lives and other's lives in many ways and hopefully reflect his love for us in the hearts of those who see it.

> *"Trouble and anguish have overtaken me, yet Your commandments are my delights"*
>
> *(Psalms 119:143).*

Social Media Posts and Emails

Wakefield Cancer Update—10.10.11 I prayed that the port placement would go well with minimal discomfort; God is faithful as it was so. Even if it had not gone well, God is still faithful. Looking forward to Sunday when some of my female family and friends will get together with me as I "de-hair." Chemo starts on Monday. Okay, Lord, you have put before me a path I have just begun to trod, may you be glorified, may I not get discouraged when the path is rough, and may I always remember that I am not alone as I take each step! (For you promise to always be with me). I hope everyone has an amazing day!

Chapter 8

A Hairy Experience

When I was young, a class picture was taken each year. It included each child in that particular class and the teacher. Also, in those days, it was rare that you actually went to a hairdresser because many households could not afford the luxury, at least not for the children. I believe it was in my second-grade year that my mother decided I needed a perm. Well, you guessed it! It was just before class pictures and it was a "home" perm. Picture this: Hair pinging in fifty million directions, hard and quirky curls that bore no resemblance to Shirley Temple's beautiful curly top. It looked like hundreds of battered corkscrews sticking out of my head. It was bad.

The kids I went to school and rode on the bus with were ruthless. I don't even remember all the different names I was called. I imagine I chose not to remember.

In those days, bullying was an accepted, though cruel, part of growing up. For a lot of children, we just went home and told "mommy," got sympathy, and went back the next day and started all over again, growing a thicker skin and the ability, over time, to defend ourselves hopefully, and unfortunately, we might recycle the abuse onto those younger or seemingly weaker than we were. I am not a proponent of bullying—just telling it like it was.

Usually though, another classmate would have some terrible "curse" brought on them by circumstances outside of their control and take the heat off us! Such things as a haircut done by a mom looking like she used a mixing bowl for a guide; trousers bought long and hemmed too short, so they could later be let out as we got taller; hand-me-down clothes and shoes; and lovingly handsewn/knitted/crocheted but fashionably uncouth clothing from relatives that had no idea what our lives would be like if we were ever to actually wear those things to school.

Being a kid is never easy, and then our parents or grandparents, aunts, uncles, and other loved ones decide to do something that unbeknownst to them makes our lives unbearable. Most times it dealt with our appearance in one way or another.

Growing into a woman, I became increasingly more concerned and passionate about my looks. I was not pretty like some other girls. I had a "flat" face (my nose is very short and didn't protrude much beyond my chin and my forehead). Yes, indeed, "flatface" was my nickname for many years until my nose started to grow a bit and contoured my face in a more pleasant form. I am not sure if my continual pulling on my nose helped it to emerge from its facial pocket or if my nose got sick of the teasing too!

I was a little overweight, another source of cruel and unusual punishment from the other kids. My hair, except for those times when my mom or aunt had "great" ideas about it, was a pretty brown color. As many young ladies, I spent a lot of time washing it, brushing it, styling it, twirling it, and paying more attention to it than was actually necessary.

A woman's hair is her adornment. One of the first things we notice about a woman is her hair. Why else would we spend so much time and money taking care of it? We have favorite hairdressers, shampoos, conditioners, hairsprays, mousses, styling gels, dyes, highlights, extensions, curling irons when our hair is too straight, and straightening irons when our hair is too curly. We have favorite hats, scarves (Does anyone wear these anymore?), clips, hair bands, scrunchies, ribbons (I am showing my age here), sparkles, spray colors, feathers, and beads. We pine over colors that were never meant to be used in hair.

As I have grown older, I have gotten a bit lazy about my hair, not wanting to spend much time on it, just wash-and-go styles are my favorite. It has a slight wave, and so, I have benefited from not needing to do a lot with it for it to look even halfway decent.

Since my chemotherapy drugs were going to cause me to lose my hair, I decided not to go through the tedium of waking up to hair falling out all over my pillowcases and sheets, clogs in the shower drain, and perhaps embarrassing losses while out and about, and essentially just prolonging the inevitable. I would take care of the issue in one sitting. I figured if we are going to do this, we might as well have fun while we were at it! Terri's "Unhairy" party planning was on a roll. Celebrating dehairing was mentioned to me by someone I work with, so I cannot take credit for the idea, but I want to thank my cosurvivor for sharing the splendid idea with me.

Who to invite; what to do; what to eat; what games to play? Cassie, Heather, and I began discussing and planning. I wanted to do this just before treatment so that I wouldn't have to keep shaving before the chemo drugs made it official.

We decided upon the weekend before chemo would start. Invitations were delivered to around twenty of my closest female friends and family. Refreshments would include "bald" eggs, "unfuzzy" navels (our bald and virgin blend of orange and pineapple juice), finger sandwiches, breast-cancer ribbon cookies, and cupcakes decorated with various stages of baldness.

We developed a couple of games based on famous people with bald heads and breast-cancer facts versus fiction. Of course, the main attraction was the actual head shaving. Heather had decided to also shave her head. My daughter Cassie and two of my grandchildren, Kurt and Robbie, chose to dye parts of their hair pink.

After the introductions, sharing, games, and food came the reason we were gathering. Heather and I sat beside each other in the kitchen. Heather's son, Kurt, was to do his mother's hair, and Cassie was going to do mine. We would start by scissor cutting the bulk of the hair and then use shavers to finish the job. I did have mental pictures of a bald head with those little pieces of tissue with the red center that I sometimes saw on my husband's head and face when he finished shaving. Due to the skilled hands we were in, the tissue was safe.

Everyone gathered around to watch us make light of what was happening, pick on each other, and give instructions to those who ultimately had our lives in their hands: "You aren't close to her ear, are you?" "These scissors aren't sharp enough!" "Those are sharp razors, aren't they?" "Okay, all you taking pictures are having way too much fun at our expense!"

As I sat there, it didn't really dawn on me how I would feel about this when it was all over. Again, I was taking it a step at a time. Finally, the floor was turning dark brown and reality was setting in. Was it too late to grab some *Superglue*? Our friends are starting to gather elsewhere to talk, and only a few stayed where they were to provide continued moral support and a healthy dose of ribbing.

After shiny new heads were cleaned and dried, we were having our own fashion show with all the hats and scarves that had come as presents and some that we had purchased. While we were doing that, the dying was taking place in the kitchen. Cassie, Kurt, and Robbie were turning various shades of pink in certain sections of their hair. A picture was sent via cellphone that four male friends and family who were getting together at another house had also shaved their heads in support, of course, that made me cry.

We were having fun, hair was swept off the floor, pictures were snapped, hats were paraded, and people started saying goodbye and heading home. Soon, it was just me, Cassie, Heather, Kurt, Robbie, and my very best friend in the whole wide world, Patty.

Patty took my hand and said, "Okay, let's go look." I hesitated. I realized then that I had been avoiding this. It was one thing to sit in a chair and have your head turned into a cue ball, but quite another to look at it! You see, I had a feeling I would look like the Addams Family's Uncle Fester, and I had actually hoped I would be alone for the first look, but my friend knew that I should not be alone and should have support when I looked for the first time. And she would not take no for an answer! I rattled off excuses, but no one was listening to them. Off to the bathroom mirror we headed. When I moved closer to the mirror, I closed my eyes. The realization that the "fun" was over and that I had been stuffing my dread for this moment was clear. They were telling me to look, but it was really difficult. I pleaded with the Lord to help me to do this.

Slowly, I allowed my eyes to open and guess what—I did look like Uncle Fester! My mother would have been having a ball (no pun intended) with the situation, so why couldn't I? I was wearing a black pantsuit, and I really did look like the Addams Family uncle, perhaps without his makeup, but really, it was a very close resemblance. Of course, they all said I didn't, but that is all I saw in the mirror—haunting eyes looking back at me. Being larger in size, all I saw was this huge head that was exposed for the world to see.

I hate bringing attention to myself, but with a bald head, you are probably going to get looked at, especially by children! It was just a shock. They all said that I had a beautifully shaped head and that I was beautiful. Inside, I knew they meant it, and probably in a few days, I might feel it too. In their presence, I made light of it and laughed and cried at the irony of it all. Before long, the children and my friend also took their leave of me.

Alone, I was afraid to go back to the bathroom. *"Not just yet,"* I said, *"let's wait awhile. Maybe the next time, I will look a little different, and it won't seem so bad, huge, scary, shiny—did I say huge—white, round, and yes, huge."* I knew a shower was in order to get rid of those prickly hairs that had gone down under my top, but I kept putting it off. The mirror was right across from the shower.

My dogs, Lexie and Princess, didn't seem to mind a bit. They still knew my voice and even lapped my face and head, letting me know it was okay. Keith wanted a picture, and so, a picture was sent by one of my daughters. He texted me how beautiful I was and that now we were twins. He was bald too by choice long before I got breast cancer. I had to admit that upon looking at the picture, I didn't look like Uncle Fester any longer. I now looked like Frosty the Snowman without his hat and pipe.

All in all, the party was good-natured fun and really did help to take what could have been a very emotional and depressing and protracted experience and turn it into just another step in the process.

With each new day, it did get easier to look at myself, and pretty soon, I did see the beauty without the hair. Eventually, with the familiarity, came a normalness and even an appreciation that though my head looked different, I was still the same Terri inside, learning, growing, stretching, and becoming stronger in faith with each new awareness.

I think back now and smile. As is the case so many times in life, we experience something that at the time seems uncomfortable or traumatic, and later on, we look back and think that it wasn't that bad after all. Being bald is one of those things. It really was not that bald…oh, sorry…bad after all.

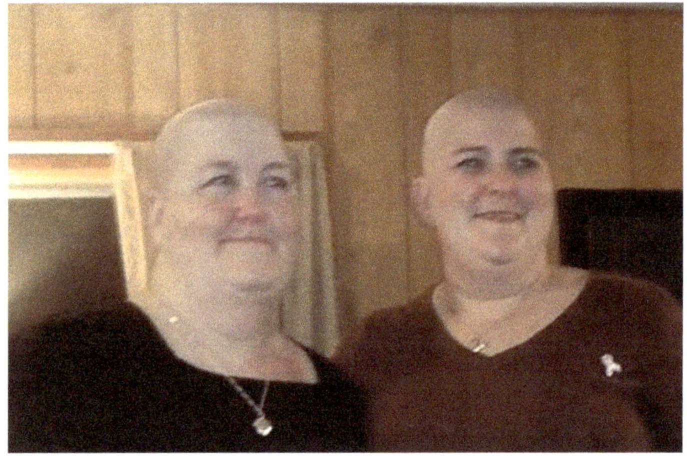

> *"But we all, with unveiled face, beholding as in a mirror the glory of the Lord, are being transformed into the same image from glory to glory, just as by the Spirit of the Lord"*
>
> *(2 Corinthians 3:18).*

10.01.11 Email: God you have ordered my steps…I am content in your path. Next steps: I saw the medical oncologist on Friday. He definitely recommends dose-dense chemotherapy for sixteen weeks, every other week, which will probably start in two to three weeks. I will definitely lose my hair and so we are planning an "Unhairy" party. My port (what they will use to give me the chemo and from which they will draw blood; much better then getting pricked each time) will be placed through day surgery on Friday, October 7th in the a.m. I have to have a MUGA heart scan (to make sure my heart is functioning okay since at least one of the chemotherapy drugs can affect heart function) this Monday morning (10/03) along with chemotherapy teaching. After the chemotherapy will be 6-1/2 weeks of radiation therapy and then five years of hormone therapy (a pill every day).

A candid discussion with the oncologist and the nurse, who also had breast cancer and went through this process, related "It is going to be tough," but it will be worth it as it raises survival rates from 50% to 75% in ten years. However, no two people respond the same way to chemotherapy, and so I remain hopeful but realistic. Dose-dense therapy means that one does not have the usual two weeks to recover from the chemotherapy since it is given every other week. Blood counts will be watched carefully. Whatever God chooses to allow will also include his grace to endure—what a lovely promise!

Your continued thoughts and prayers that my ability to work during chemotherapy will not be greatly affected are appreciated. The doctor feels that I may need to move to very part-time during the four months of chemo, but he said I could work what I felt good enough to do. Thanks so much!

10.10.11 Email: An Unhairy Party

When: Sunday, October 16, at 4:00 p.m.

Where: Terri Wakefield's home at 15 Maple Acres, Waterford. Directions below.

Why: Celebrating Terri's de-hairing! Snacks and drinks provided.

Wakefield Cancer Journal 10.01.11: God you have ordered my steps...I am content in your path. Next steps: Dose-dense chemotherapy for sixteen weeks, every other week. I will definitely lose my hair and so we are planning an "Unhairy" party. After the chemotherapy will be 6-1/2 weeks of radiation therapy and then five years of hormonal therapy. October is Breast Cancer Awareness Month. Your continued prayers that my ability to work during chemotherapy will not be greatly affected are appreciated. Will you pray with me? Thanks so much!

Bible Blessings

Boldness from Baldness (from my devotional Bible for Women). I really identified with this devotional as it talked about how God uses the cancer not to slow down but to accelerate our desire for others to know the truth and grace about him. I know my heart's desire has been that people realize that cancer is just one of the journeys that God may put us through to not only draw us to him but to draw others to him as well. I want people to see that by his grace he doesn't take away the bad stuff from our lives, but that he gives us the grace and the support (from him and others he uses) to get through it and come out on the other side blessed more than we could ever have been without the experience. I am really excited to perhaps one day write a short story or be able to share somehow my experience that may be an encouragement to others.

Chapter 9

Would You Like Nuts with that Chemo?

That dreaded term—chemo. It conjures up thoughts of pain, uncontrollable nausea, loss of hair, and diminished quality of life. Once I knew that chemotherapy was recommended, I, too, felt the same dread. But I also knew, just through the type of work I do, that there have been many advances, not only in the chemotherapy drugs themselves but also in the medicines, supplements, and other treatments that can lessen the impact of chemotherapy symptoms on our body.

Even after all these years of research and technological and medical advances, we still fear this treatment—perhaps reasonably so. Or are we letting the past experiences of others shape our mindset about the present?

The effects can differ depending on the type of cancer being treated, the drugs needed as well as their side effects, and the length of the therapy that is recommended. My body's reaction may not, and probably will not, be anything like someone else's experience or, then again, it may be similar.

The day had come: A bright, sunny day with wisps of clouds and the crispness of fall. I had received chemotherapy teaching and been told what to expect—though everyone is different, they say—and so, I did not arrive at the infusion center with anxiety or fear, but with what I would call a nervous anticipation. What would it be like? How long would it take? Could my daughters go in with me? Does everyone talk to each other? What is the mood like? Will it hurt? Will I feel funny during the infusion? Will the port work? Will I be able to go to the potty? What I may experience after the chemotherapy was purposely not what I was going to think about at this point; that would come in its own good time.

It would have been nice, I suppose, to have had a tour of the infusion center to get a little insight as to what goes on. I am one of those people who like to know what to expect. However, a tour was not done, probably for patient confidentiality reasons, and I arrived for my premiere session looking my very best, one of my new hats on my clean-shaved head, with a smile, and determined not to be overwhelmed by whatever happened.

I checked in and waited to be called. There were a few others in the waiting room who I could tell were at various stages of treatment, some with a full head of hair and me with none. One was in a wheelchair and others looked very athletic and healthy. That was the reality—every person is different and there is no cookie-cutter approach to treatment or to outcome. It also finally sunk in that this was an infusion center and not everyone that comes through these doors is suffering from cancer. Some are battling blood disorders and other diseases that require regular intravenous infusions. I would never have answers to my guessing game, but that doesn't mean I couldn't use my imagination for distraction.

The nurses were good natured and professional. They were competent and empathetic. I did notice that even though the main room was open with just curtains separating each infusion chair and equipment, most of those in the "chairs" were quiet, either watching the portable TV that accompanied each chair, reading, or talking quietly with the person who was allowed to be with them.

A few were discussing issues with the nurse. Sometimes, a social worker would come by to speak with someone. It was quite busy with most chairs filled, and yet I was struck by the quietness compared to the number of people. I wondered if everyone was thinking as I was, mulling over the events that brought us to this place. For me, I wondered what God had in store. Would he provide someone for me to talk to that needed to hear about him? There was no way to tell what he had in mind. I just had to be open to the possibilities and the possibility that I would be the only one that he would be working on during my infusion "miniexcursions."

My nurse was very pleasant and welcomed me and introduced herself, having me stop at the scale (sometimes that was the thing I dreaded the most!). Body weight is one of the criteria they use to formulate how much of the drug the patient receives. My oncologist had already placed the order for the chemotherapy. The infusion nurse communicates body weight and other information to the oncology pharmacist, who is conveniently close by and who mixes the chemotherapy solution.

With the competence that comes with repetition and the answers that come with knowing her specialty, we walked through what was to be expected in this session. My port was in place. One of my daughters was at my side and the other working at her computer in the waiting area with the plan for them to switch places once or twice.

After taking my blood pressure and pulse—both were elevated but that was not a surprise to them or me—the next thing was to access my port site to make sure it flushed well and that there was a blood return. A blood return means that the port is functioning correctly and is required by many facilities in order to receive chemotherapy. If there is no blood return, there are various maneuvers, like, lying back, turning head to the side, raising an arm, and putting an anticoagulant, such as, heparin into the port to see if that might help. They can also change the size of the needle, infuse normal saline, and/or use an agent such as Cathflo, an antithrombotic agent, to break up clots. If everything fails, it might lead to imaging studies or other procedures to see what the problem is. Well, I was one of the "lucky" ones who had problems each time, in that the blood did not want to return. In retrospect, only once did the port function without some kind of hitch. It would flush well but did not want to give any blood back. On almost every visit, I had to receive the Cathflo, which would extend my visit, since it would often take one to two hours to work. I was often in the infusion center for up to four or four and a half hours.

Later on, the surgeon explained that he felt that the negative pressure of the withdrawal of blood caused the catheter to move to the side of the vein, and the holes in the catheter were getting blocked, so the blood could not be pulled back through. However, during the infusion, that was not the case, and the catheter functioned normally.

While I was waiting on my first day for the antithrombotic to work, I enjoyed the view outside the window across from my very comfortable chair. As I said earlier, the sky was a brilliant blue with a few wispy paint strokes of white and mossy-colored tree tops jutting up and intersecting the sky on the horizon. The view relaxed me. I imagined what it would be like to be a soaring raptor enjoying a ride on the wind and playing in the vast openness with my eye on whatever interested me. That would be much more fun than sitting where I was.

By the time my blood decides to come out of hiding and excite us by its presence, the infusion bags are mixed and ready. The skin over the port is numbed with a freezing spray and the infusion needle is pushed through my skin into the PowerPort underneath, and I become tethered to the cancer-fighting drugs that will hopefully kill any menacing cancer cells that may still remain inside me.

My questions were quickly answered either by the nurse or by observation, listening, and the staff's interaction with other patients. I could go to the bathroom if I needed to; just take the bag and the pole and roll on down the aisle. We probably could come up with a cute little jingle about that—maybe another time.

Time went slowly at some points and quickly at others. I guess it depended on whether I was engaged in something outside of myself or I was being introspective, and thoughts were all about me. Specific prayers were shot up, and I trusted that other more I-am-depending-on-the-Holy-Spirit-to-know-what-I-need-and-intercede-for-me prayers were happening without me being aware of them.

The session was finally over with absolutely no side effects felt. Since I lived quite a distance from the hospital and from my usual shopping haunts, we generally stopped for something to eat and got groceries and anything else we needed. I did notice that, even after the first session, there was a fatigue that came on more quickly than usual. By the time I got home, I was ready for a nap or bed for the night.

First Cycle

It generally took about two days for symptoms, other than the fatigue, to rear their ugly heads (yes, they had bald heads too). With my first round, my appetite was suppressed, not usually because of nausea, but just suppressed. We tried to come up with different higher-calorie food items for me to ingest, as was suggested, but nothing sounded good. I had no interest in eating. Once in a great while, I would feel hungry, but the thought of actually eating would soon kill the hunger.

My caretaker for the day would cajole, push, manipulate, threaten, and eventually just plain give up on me eating much of anything. I tried, but when you have an aversion to putting something in your mouth, it just ain't gonna happen! The upside was I hoped I would lose some weight; the downside was I didn't.

"What's up with that," I wondered.

Though nausea was a battle during the first couple of sessions, I realized that if I took the antinausea and antiemetic medications around the clock—setting alarms for the middle of the night—that nausea was minimal. I only had one bout of vomiting which happened after my first session before I had found the right timing regimen for taking the medication.

Having the chemotherapy every other week gave me about five days between sessions when I felt pretty good and functioned pretty close to normal. I still was tired, but I was able to work my job taking only minimal time off, usually being able to make up some of that time during the normal days. Work was a good distraction. It made me feel like the cancer and its treatment did not have power over me, that I had power over it to some degree.

I got to say when I felt like working. Many times, I worked when I didn't feel like it just because it would help me forget that I was not feeling very well. Things seemed normal, sort of. However, the price my employers paid was that my mind was not always clear. I have heard this is called "chemobrain". I didn't even realize it until it was over. Looking back, I saw that my mind was not as sharp, it took me longer to figure things out, to look things up, to troubleshoot and problem solve. It happened so gradually that I didn't really notice it, but when it was gone, I could definitely tell the difference. This particular side effect doesn't happen to everyone; and if it does happen, it can vary in its intensity.

Though I was somewhat forgetful before, just a part of aging I think, this illness and its treatment magnified it. I think most of the people who interacted with me on a regular basis wished that they could paste sticky notes all over my body to remind me of things I needed to do, people I needed to call, and other things like go to bed, wake up and breathe. Okay, I am exaggerating. Unfortunately, as I write this, the memory thing has stayed the same or worsened. I want to blame it on cancer and its treatment, but truthfully the current memory issues may or may not be related. The timing is suspicious—very suspicious—at least I think it is, that is, if I am remembering correctly.

As was expected, I did experience some generalized bone pain, more of an ache like I had been walking around a store all day, but nothing really painful and resting helped.

And there was the hair loss, I mean *everywhere*. Under my arms, pubic region, eye lashes, eyebrows, legs, arms, facial hair, even the hair on my toes! I equate it to being a shriveled up newborn baby.

Second Cycle

Blue pee! Sounds like an idea for an adult version of a Dr. Seuss story. This was my very first side effect from paclitaxel. They told me to expect it, but blue is not what you think you will find on the toilet paper after going to the bathroom. Then to stand up, turn around to flush, and for a moment think that someone must have been cleaning the throne before I took my rightful place upon it. Oops, it is not those scrubbing blue bubbles; it is me. Wow, it is a pretty shade of blue. Anyone got a camera? My friends are going to think this is a blue fish story.

Some of the side effects of this cycle were familiar. I was still tired all the time, and my stamina was low. My appetite was still nil. However, there were other reactions that were different: Bone pain and peripheral neuropathy, namely, numbness and tingling in the hands and feet. I remember the first day that the bone pain started. It was about three to four days after my chemotherapy session. I was lying on the couch watching television. My right ankle started to hurt; first, it was a mild ache, but within an hour, the pain had increased to real pain that was extending up my right leg, and it spread to the other side.

I called the oncologist's office right away knowing that I was going to need something to help the pain, because by this time, nothing was taking my mind off how much it hurt.

The nurse told me that I should take some Claritin, an over-the-counter antihistamine for seasonal-type allergies, because this can sometimes be helpful. I told her that Claritin was not going to work and that I needed *strong* drugs! She got my drift, and soon the doctor had called in a prescription, which fortunately helped a lot. After two sessions, I noticed that the pain started on day three after chemo and usually lasted three to four days and then eased up and stopped completely. Again, I found the proactive approach worked best.

On the third day after chemo, I would start first thing in the morning by taking one pain pill. After taking one pill every four hours two times, I would do two pills every four hours. By doing this, the bone pain, though present, was very manageable. After a couple of days, there was absolutely no pain, and I would reduce to one pill every seven to eight hours, and if still no pain, I would stop.

It was around this same time that I started noticing that I was stumbling a bit, tripping over my feet and that my fingertips would feel "funny." Not really a prickly sensation and not totally numb, but just a funny, unusual sensation that was annoying at worst. I found it increasingly difficult to hold onto small items and had a hard time picking up something flat, like, a coin, from a flat surface.

Sometimes when standing up, I would sway like a drunken sailor. It raised a few eyebrows. My sense of balance was being thrown off by the diminished sensation in my feet.

I had been admonished by the chemotherapy teaching nurse to take a supplement called L-glutamine which usually helped to minimize peripheral neuropathy symptoms and to keep them from becoming permanent. I bought the L-glutamine at a health food store. It had a gritty kind of consistency, and I found it was most palatable in a glass of milk. However, it was still a little difficult to get down.

My patient and loving daughters did their best to get that stuff into me—and usually I was pretty good about it. However, if you ask them, they will probably give you a different side to the story, so don't ask them; I like my take on it. At this point in my journey, getting anything past my lips was a definite victory. The blessing was that I still have minor neuropathy in my feet, but nothing like I had at that time.

My last day of chemotherapy was one of differing feelings. I was glad to have it over with, but yet, I wondered if I had received enough. Did the amount I had taken in get it all? I also felt like the worst was over and that I was on the downhill side of my cancer treatment, a place that seemed like I would never get to, but was glad that it had finally arrived.

I had already started the planning for the next step of the journey—radiation therapy. That should be a breeze…

> *For I know the thoughts that I think toward you, says the Lord, thoughts of peace and not of evil, to give you a future and a hope. Then you will call upon Me and go and pray to Me, and I will listen to you. And you will seek Me and find Me when you search for Me with all your heart. I will be found by you, says the Lord, and I will bring you back from your captivity.*
>
> *(Jeremiah 29:11–14a)*

Social Media Posts and Emails

Wakefield Cancer Update 10.17.11: Had first chemo session today. Went well. Sat by a big window with beautiful blue sky and puffy white clouds: Thank you, Lord, you knew what I needed to relax. Reminded me of when I was a little girl and laid on the lawn looking up at the sky. God your creation is amazing! It also helped to have Cassie and Heather with me for support. Went shopping at Wal-Mart after. Only had one queasy moment this evening and took an antinausea medication. Have to go back in tomorrow for a Neulasta shot to boost my white cells. Ho-hum, got to love it!!!! Thanks everyone for your wonderful well wishes, thoughts and prayers. They all mean so much to me!

Lord, thank you for a beautiful time at my "Unhairy" party; I was joined by eighteen friends and family. My daughter Heather also shaved her head (she is the pretty one on the right), my daughter Cassie dyed her hair pink, my grandson shaved his head, my granddaughter dyed some of her hair pink. There were so many pictures being taken I thought I was on the red carpet! Also, some male friends shaved their heads and painted breast-cancer ribbons on the side. Need to find that photo! Lots of fun, lots of pink. We drank unfuzzy navels, ate bald eggs and hairy cupcakes along with other good stuff. Thanks everyone for making the day memorable!

A Cancer Patient Speaks:

What can you do or say to offer support for me?

Be honest with me. I can tell when your feelings or actions are insincere.

Laugh with me, cry with me. Allow me to express intense emotions.

Don't feel sorry for me. Your understanding helps preserve my dignity and pride. Touch me. I want to be accepted despite the way I look. Inside I'm still the same person you always knew. Let me talk about my illness if I want to. Talking helps me work through my feelings. Let me be silent if I want to. Sometimes I don't have much energy and I just want your silent companionship. Your presence alone can be comforting. Space your visits and calls. Consistent support is very helpful. Support my family. I may be sick, but they, too, are suffering. Give them an opportunity to express their feelings. —taken from a hospice newsletter.

10.18.11: Heather sent me Martina McBride video "I'm going to love you through it."

"...When you're weak, I'll be strong
When you let go, I'll hold on
When you need to cry, I swear
That I'll be there to dry your eyes
When you feel lost and scared to death,
Like you can't take one more step
Just take my hand, together we can do it
I'm gonna love you through it.
And when this road gets too long
I'll be the rock you lean on
Just take my hand, together we can do it
I'm gonna love you through it.
I'm gonna love you through it..."

Wakefield Cancer Update 10.20.11: Well it hasn't been terrible! Nausea comes in little waves but medication helps. Some bone pain. Lots of fatigue. All expected. God is good. The thing about sleeping so much: Someone else does your dishes!

Wakefield Cancer Update 10.28.11: What a wonderful week I have had!! Thank you Lord for giving me a reprieve, allowing me to get some much-needed housework and personal organization done. We start another round on Monday, but having the week in between to feel good and be able to work and get some personal stuff done is just wonderful! God is so good; I am so blessed. Everyone's prayers are making such a difference...thank you for that friends and family!

Wakefield Cancer Update 11.02.11. Chemo yesterday and I wasn't bothered as much with fatigue and nauseousness as I was the last time on the night of chemo. However, I did develop a new side effect though it is minimal at this point: Peripheral neuropathy (when your hands and feet have tingling and prickly feeling and/or pain). We were blessed that my Neulasta shot will be able to be given at home. Cassie and Heather have learned how to do that and the copay on that $5000 shot is only $30—Praise the Lord! This will save making another trip to the city the day after chemo. I continue to be blessed with cards, hats, chocolates and other gifts (too numerous to mention). Sometimes it makes me cry (good tears) as they often come during sadder moments—God's rainbow that he often sends just after the rain in our lives.

11.02.11 Email: Hello everyone,

I am still getting cards, hats, flowers, chocolates, etc., and am very happy that my friends are supporting in that manner. I also know there are probably 100+ people praying for me (all across the country), and that is making this journey so much easier. I read about horror stories of what some people have gone through and just bless the Lord everyday that I am not having some of those harrowing experiences (yet anyway and if they come...well that will be okay too because I know I am not alone).

My second chemotherapy was yesterday (it was supposed to be Monday but there was a scheduling snafu). Last time I had lots of nausea and very tired, even the first night. Yesterday was not as bad. I had asked the oncologist what my cumulative effects might be, and he said nausea and fatigue. I was able to work 8 hours last night which was great. Did get a little tired but was determined to make it through.

I did notice one more side effect that is coming on—peripheral neuropathy. That is when the chemo drugs affect the nerves in your hands and feet. I woke up with pins and needles in my right hand and thought I just slept wrong; but I noted it throughout the night intermittently in both hands. I will call the oncologist today and inform them as they have instructed patients to do that.

We have been in contact with the oncology social worker and she has informed us about possible resources. We are applying for assistance from the hospital for the $5000 deductible which we would have to pay. We are also applying through another cancer foundation for $800 assistance that could go toward heat, transportation, medical bills, etc., and we have decided to put it toward heat assistance should we get it. We have also applied for another smaller grant of $100 from another cancer foundation that you can use for whatever is needed.

I believe I have mentioned before that 24 hours after chemotherapy (can't be done any sooner) I need to have a Neulasta shot. This shot helps to lessen the chance of infection by boosting the number of white cells in the system. This was a bit of a burden having to go to the city 2 days in a row, especially in the wintertime. So we were able to get a preauthorization from the insurance company to give the shot at home, and both my daughters, Cassie and Heather, were shown how to administer it. (Now I will have to be extra sweet so they won't be tempted to "just stick it anywhere." I then was concerned of how much the copay would be on a shot that cost $5000. Yep, you heard it right, $5000 each. I called the insurance company and with a really sad voice, she let me know that the copay was only $30. Wow, another blessing. The copays alone on these and every office visit are very draining so this was a huge blessing.

11.15.11: God's rainbows—you know, the unexpected gift, the encouraging note or phone call, the interaction with another who has been touched by you, the blessing we receive when we can do for others, and especially the blessings from God received for no other reason than because we are loved by Him—God use me as a rainbow in someone's life today, so that they may know that you are a personal God, a loving God, a righteous God, a just God, you are always there for us and give us just what we need.

It has been fun wearing different hats; however, now that my face is a bit pale, I need to do the earrings and makeup so I don't look like the walking dead!!! It has put some fun into the process!

I also have never been "looked at" as much as I have lately. I am flat chested and bald. My friend made me some knitted boobies, which are wonderful but tend to migrate in my sports bra so I have not worn them as much as I would like. (I need to get a bra that has the pockets.) Last Sunday I was in church and one of our friends (male of course) decided to take my arm on an extended exercise hello, shaking my hand like there was no tomorrow. I finally asked him to slow down because my boob was migrating (I could feel it moving toward the middle of my chest). He is hard of hearing and I don't think he realized he probably heard me correctly (it was funny!) as he had this really confused look on his face. I almost whipped out the thing to show him but decided they might throw me out of the church for being indecent so decided against it. PS: I hope no one takes offense of my verbiage here, but not sure what better way to express the reality and the humor (which is really important right now.)

Every day there seems to be something to smile or laugh about and I am so grateful to God and my friends for making it so!

Wakefield Cancer Update 01.03.12—Only 2 more chemo sessions to go!!!! Yeah. Thank you Lord as you continue to be with me on this journey. Thank you to my daughters, Cassie and Heather, for going with me to my sessions, keeping me company. The new chemotherapy infusions are very long. Yesterday was at the infusion center for

5-1/2 hours. My port is less cooperative with each session, delaying the start of the 3-hour infusion because although they can put stuff into the port, the blood will not return right away and they cannot start the chemo drugs unless there is blood return; they also check my blood counts with the blood return. They now have to put in CathFlo which is a special drug that will help get the blood to come out of the port, but we have to wait for that to work (half hour to 45 minutes). Hopefully this port will hold up for 2 more sessions!! Although there is little nausea with this new chemo drug, there is the difficult side effect of bone and muscle pain that starts a day or two after treatment and lasts about 3 days. Next month will start radiation therapy for 6-1/2 weeks. Thank you to all my friends who continue to support me with prayers, thoughts, emails, cards, etc. They lift me up!!!! Love to you all.

Wakefield Cancer Update 12.3.11—Update: That usually infers that something has changed; however, in my case thankfully not much has in the way of treatment/condition. As I was thinking of writing an update and nothing much coming to mind to report on, the Lord reminded me that it is true that nothing much has changed BUT that is because He has continued to be watching over me, sustaining me, helping me, reminding me, refreshing me, listening to me, and most of all loving me. The only minor thing to report is that this week has been the toughest yet with an increase in the peripheral neuropathy and a couple of bouts with vomiting; it still could be so much worse, that I feel truly blessed by God's loving care and all your prayers of support.

01.04.12 Email: Only 2 more chemo sessions to go!!!! Yeah. Thank you Lord as you continue to be with me on this journey and for preparing me for whatever you have for me after that. Thank you to my daughters, Cassie and Heather, for going with me to my sessions and doctor appointments, keeping me company, and taking care of me at home during chemo week. They make sure I don't forget my medicine and supplements, they cook for me, they clean up after themselves (I like that one). Thank you to my son Toby who always does me any favors when I need them. Thanks to Jennie, my daughter in California, who writes me notes to encourage me.

The new chemotherapy infusions are very long. This past Monday, I was at the infusion center for 5-1/2 hours. My port is less cooperative with each session, delaying the start of the 3-hour chemo infusion because although they can put the drugs into the port, the blood will not return right away and they cannot start the chemo drugs unless there is a blood return; they also check my blood counts with the blood return. They now have to put in CathFlo which is a special drug that will help to get the blood to come out of the port, but we have to wait for that to work (30 to 45 minutes). Hopefully this port will hold up for 2 more sessions!!! Although there is little nausea with this new chemo drug, there is the difficult side effect of bone and muscle pain that starts a day or two after treatment and lasts for about 3 days.

Next month will start radiation therapy daily for 6-1/2 weeks. I am still working on getting everything together so I can actually stay at the Arbor House (which is next to the hospital). The house does not have Internet access which I definitely need to work. My own cell company and cable company do not offer mobile Internet, and so am checking out another route. If that all fails, I might try to find someone in the Lewiston-Auburn area that would be willing to let me stay with them for that time, or I will just make the trip daily (which I was trying to avoid to save gas, wear and tear on car, winter traveling, etc.)

Sometimes I feel like I am getting "chemobrain": As Ashleigh Brilliant once said, "My mind contains many good ideas, but it's not always easy to squeeze one out." Boy I have those kind of days once in a while.

Thank you to all my family and friends who continue to support me with prayers, thoughts, emails, cards, etc. They lift me up!!!! Love to you all.

Wakefield Cancer update 01.06.12—Just a little bit of further update. Saw oncologist today. Things going well. Does not need to see me til 02/08. Red counts down a bit causing some shortness of breath but not enough to take the Neulasta (yeah). Bone pain is present and sometimes difficult, but I am blessed because I know it could be worse. Meet with radiation therapist on 02/08.

01.17.12: 1 Corinthians 12:10—"Therefore I am well content with weaknesses, with insults, with distresses, with persecutions, with difficulties, for Christ's sake; for when I am weak, then I am strong." Our weaknesses really allow God's strength to become evident (when we don't try to do it in our own strength). I am so grateful for God's grace and provision.

Wakefield Cancer Update 01.17.12: Chemo today. They decided to do a 25% dose reduction to the Taxol chemotherapy. They are concerned that the peripheral neuropathy, leg and arm pain and weakness could become permanent. On the previous infusion, the symptoms lasted a week. Just one more chemo session to go. The port worked a bit better today, didn't have to wait as long for blood return. Blood counts "looked good" they said. Praise the Lord and you for your prayers and support. Felt wonderful to be with my church family on Sunday!

Made my reservations at the Arbor House (right across from CMMC) to stay there while I have radiation therapy for 6-1/2 weeks. That should start in mid-February. I see the radiation oncologist on 02/08, and they may do the simulation/mapping that day, and I suspect the therapy will start the week after. I believe we have worked out the Internet details for my work but continue to pray that that process will go smoothly. If that doesn't work out, I will have no choice but to travel back and forth daily or find someone in the Lewiston area that has high-speed Internet available that would allow me to stay with them (due to the confidentiality of the work I do, it would have to be a private area in someone's home).

I just want to take a moment to thank God for my wonderful family who have been sooooooo supportive during this time, offering to help with either caretaking right after chemotherapy, shoveling in the snow storms, offering to help with transportation when I am too weak to drive, cooking, cleaning, encouraging, admonishing, loving me no matter what, as well as practical/financial assistance. My friends have encouraged and lightened my heart with many cards, emails, and phone calls with offers to help and letting me know of their care and support (or just to listen when I need to whine).

I Corinthians 12:10—*"Therefore I am well content with weaknesses, with insults, with distresses, with persecutions, with difficulties, for Christ's sake; for when I am weak, then I am strong."* Our weaknesses really allow God's strength to become evident (when we don't try to do it in our own strength). I am so grateful for God's grace and provision.

God bless you all!

01.22.12: My daughters surprised me (along with my grandson) with a wonderful (it was great!) fish fry (haddock) today for my birthday. Along with homemade cole slaw, French fries, and caramel brownies. It was great. I still have some to "snack" on. One of the greatest birthday presents ever—food! Love you guys!

Wakefield Cancer Update 01.24.12—My birthday (the 23rd) was spent not feeling well physically but knowing that I am truly blessed to be loved by our Creator and to be loved and cared for by many family and friends. This current chemo drug continues to give side effects that are difficult and last longer, but knowing there is only 1 more infusion lightens the heart!

01.29.12: Hey FB Friends! I really need some prayer today. Have come down with cold that has moved to my chest. Doing what I can to push fluids and rest. Infusion center said I could have chemo tomorrow if I don't have a fever, so praying that is the case. Thanks everyone!

Wakefield Cancer Update 01.30.12: Well I did not have chemo today. I did go to the infusion center and my counts were good, no fever, good oxygenated blood; but because

I have been coughing up yellowish sputum, they decided to put me on an antibiotic (Z-Pak) and reschedule my chemo for Friday. Even though I wanted today to be it...I certainly trust their judgment and know this is for the best so the chemo doesn't inhibit my getting better from the cold. God is good: All the time! Thanks to all of you who prayed for no fever...I didn't get one...and appreciate all your words of encouragement! XOXOXOXOXOXOXOXO

Chapter 10

When Things Heat Up

January 2012

The hard part was over—chemotherapy was done! The major last leg of my journey was radiation therapy. I met with the radiation oncologist pretty early on, and she thoroughly reviewed the treatment, process, side effects, and duration:

Radiation therapy to the chest wall (skin and muscle left behind after surgery), lymph nodes in the right axillary area and the right neck for twenty-five treatments over five weeks. Then, I would have radiation treatment only to the incision scar for eight treatments over one and a half weeks, for a total of six and a-half weeks. The actual treatment session was less than five minutes; I would be in and out of the unit in twenty minutes.

The short-term side effects to radiation therapy would include skin reaction, like, "a sunburn," patchy and maybe itchy, and most certainly with blisters. These could be treated with local creams, steroids and pain medication if necessary. Longer-term side effects could include radiation pneumonia, discoloration to the skin, arm swelling, shortness of breath, and cough; some of which also could be treated if they developed.

I was told that without radiation, there was a thirty percent chance of the cancer coming back locally, but with radiation, it was reduced to five percent.

Plans for simulation were made where they figure out where exactly they are going to direct the radiation and scheduled me for my tattooing. I will forever have a reminder of my radiation treatment. I have a pencil-tip-sized tattoo on my upper mid chest and two on my sides. These were where the radiation therapists would line up the machine that would deliver the radiation beam.

I was convinced that radiation would be no big deal. After all, chemo is what everyone seems to dread and talk about with much consternation. My feeling was to get this waypoint finished, so I could continue on with the journey of life, whatever God had in mind for my future.

This segment of the course was a logistical problem. I lived forty-five minutes from the center, and it was winter in Maine—not a good combination! Going back and forth every weekday for over six weeks could be quite challenging, especially with winter storms, ice, and probable weather delays. We decided that since Keith was on the road and my daughters were working, I would "move" into the *Arbor House*, the hospitality house, directly across the street from the radiation treatment center.

Since I had a full-time job working from home, my desk, computer, chair, and printer would have to accompany me. I confirmed with the hospitality house that this would be allowed. The thermostat at my home in the boonies was turned down; the dogs were visiting with relatives for the duration; and a moving day was scheduled.

There was enough to move that we commandeered a pickup truck and thank the Lord it was not snowing. They gave me a big room, so it was very comfortable with the office furniture and a full-sized bed, two chairs, sink, bathroom, and television. Hey, I was on vacation—yeah, right!

There was a common kitchen and lounge area, but my work/sleep schedule kept me inside my room most of the time. There was daily housekeeping and a laundry on site. It was in the middle of the city and unfortunately less than a block from my favorite pizza and sandwich shop! I opened up a temporary mailbox and had my mail forwarded. My every-few-day mail run and my once-a-week grocery run served to break up the monotony.

It was hard dealing with being pretty much alone for the duration. There had been someone with me during each phase of my treatment process, but now, I was by myself, with no family around to ease the long stretches of loneliness.

Each day at the appointed time, I would walk a couple-hundred feet to the center. I would find an open locker, grab a gown, go change, and then wait to be called in. The waiting area before we entered the actual therapy rooms was quiet and had eight to ten chairs. As you know, I am a people watcher. Sometimes, I might see a tear running down someone's face; sometimes, I see stoic men; and other times, I see a person who looked alone and distraught. I had no idea where they were at on their journeys, and though God never led me to speak to them about him, I certainly prayed for them.

For the first few weeks, everything went well. There were minimal side effects, but I put on lotions that would keep my skin as supple as possible. I worked, I prayed, I did devotions, I watched television, I had a daily talk with my husband by phone, and I slept. That was my life for a month and a half.

One day, my daughter Cassie did come and spend the day and night with me. She decided she would not do it again. She couldn't watch TV while I slept, and she couldn't sleep while I was working. The sound of typing didn't bode well for her being able to fall or stay asleep, and my work required me to be able to listen, and so the TV didn't bode well for me to do my job effectively.

Once in a while, a friend stopped by and took me to lunch which I thoroughly enjoyed. My husband came home on two occasions while I was there and, of course, stayed with me which was wonderful. The time unfortunately was slow moving. I did have short visits from my children and Patty, my BFF.

So far, my optimism for the ease of radiation therapy was right on, but by the time we got down to the last stretch of the radiation treatment and when they were starting to do just the incision line, things changed drastically. They began to use a "bolster," which is a folded-up piece of material, a light blanket I think, that kept the radiation beam nearer to the surface. This was when things started getting interesting—very interesting. Well, maybe, "interesting" isn't the right word. The true meaning of radiation treatment hit full force, and for me, the resultant effects of the bolstering and directed treatment to the mastectomy incision line became one of the most physically challenging aspects of my entire cancer treatment.

To call it a sunburn is a massive understatement. The color of my right chest wall and upper right side was deep purplish red, blistering with grey-black skin and just a nauseating feeling when looking at it. The pain was intense. I could not move my right arm, which I used for typing or the computer mouse, without rubbing this area. My clothes rubbed it and my arm rubbed it. I am right-handed, so the area was continually being bombarded with stimulation.

Sleeping became a much sought-after time of relief, but it was not to be. I generally sleep on my side. I couldn't sleep on my right side obviously. Sleeping on my left was a bit challenging, because I had no comfortable place to put my right arm that didn't somehow involve touching and rubbing my right side.

I finally happened on two large round Ty Balls—I chose a ladybug and a bee—that had eyes that followed you wherever you moved. They were adorable and became my bedmates. I used them to put my right arm across as I kept them close to my chest. Their smiles and eyes were a bright spot in my day.

The pain and irritation finally got so bad that I begged the therapists to not use the bolster. They called in the radiation oncologist, and she agreed that I had burned enough and that we could continue on without it.

As I have mentioned earlier in my tale, at the height of the discomfort, a Sunday, I had reached the end of my physical rope. I was discouraged and deflated. However, I knew that God was there and understood. After all, he had withstood the pain of the cross; I only had a bad burn to put up with.

I went to my church family that day, to the house of God, because there was nothing else I could do. I had nothing in and of myself to make things better; there was nothing that any human could do to make it feel better. He was the only one who could take my brokenness and use it for his good.

The physical pain was very apparent on my face and in my voice. Most everyone knew that I needed a special dose of prayer—and what a difference that made.

I went back to Arbor House, feeling revived in spirit if not in body, took a refreshing nap, woke up, and went to work.

Within a few hours, I realized that the pain had lessened, and I was actually able to make up some time! Hallelujah—God had heard and answered my prayer and the prayers of my loving church family. Even now, as I recount the events of this time, tears well up because it was such a precious touch from the Lord that day that made all the difference. I am awed at how he works. I may not understand his ways or why he allows what comes my way, but I do not have to. All I have to do is trust him.

On graduation day from radiation therapy, I had been told there would be a small ceremony. I walked into the room and the two therapists who were on that day pulled out bottles of bubbles and began to blow bubbles into the air. I do not know what I was expecting, but that was not it. However, it was fitting because the bubbles of blisters on my chest would soon burst into nothingness like the bubbles being blown about the room.

God, your sense of humor amazes me! And yes, I could see Jesus blowing bubbles my way that day, rejoicing with me, with thanksgiving, that the worst was truly over.

> *"The Lord your God in your midst, The Mighty One, will save; He will rejoice over you with gladness, He will quiet you with His love, He will rejoice over you with singing."*
>
> *Zephaniah 3:17*

Wakefield Cancer Update 02.09.12: Radiation therapy mapping/simulation today, yeah...got 3 little tattoos with a couple more coming next week—I am marked!!! Therapy starts Wednesday, 02.15. I move to Arbor House (a hospital sponsored house for patients and families using the facilities for extended lengths of time) on Sunday, 02.12. Got a USB modem so should hopefully have no problems working from there. Animals are staying with family. Doctor said that this will be different than chemotherapy, probably easier, with only local skin irritation and tiredness. Went and bought my recommended aloe vera and moisturizing creams to help with the skin reaction. God, here is the next leg of the journey...and I am excited to see how you use it in my life and the life of others. Use me to be a blessing to even just one person each day. Praise: The peripheral neuropathy (tingling and numbness in hands and feet) seems to have reversed some—a big yeah God! And my hair has started growing back—some whitish grey peach fuzz up there now :) Hmmm, we'll be ready for a "rehairy" party when radiation is over! Your continued prayers are so welcome! May God bless you for keeping Him first and for your intercession on the behalf of those He puts in your minds and hearts!

Wakefield Update 02.13.12: Move to Arbor House complete. Nice big room. Mobile broadband works great—PTL! Thank you to Arthur, Linda, Cassie, Heather, Robby and Kurt for helping with the move and unpacking. Rad therapy starts Wednesday. There is only one problem: I am now just yards from Sam's Pizza! Oy vey! I have to keep reminding myself God is the author of self-control... me, not so much...

02.16.12: Nothing gets better than this: We are loved by the Creator of the universe, with such personal understanding…I mean He really gets us, our needs, our wants, our quirks, our inadequacies, our specialness…then why do we doubt that whatever happens to us is for a purpose…when we belong to Him, we have nothing to fear, even death is without fear, life is without fear. I may not always "feel" like this is true, but I certainly "know" that it is—I'll set my mind on that! I love this quote: "Anything can happen to me tomorrow, but at least nothing more can happen to me yesterday." (Ashleigh Brilliant). Have a good chuckle and a good day, my friends!!!

Wakefield Cancer Update 03.10.12—Well I am half way through my radiation therapy. It has been an interesting process and gone quicker than I imagined. I have started with the skin reaction, like a bad sunburn. I have it on the chest area on the right and then also on the right side of my neck and a place on my back. The neck and back areas are places where there is nodal drainage and so they want to treat those areas as well. I do get tired more easily, too. The treatments are quick; I am usually only in there for about 5–10 minutes. It has been a blessing to be at the Arbor House. The room is great with plenty of room for my desk, computer and chair. I do get lonely once in a while :). I go to the Dempsey Center one day a week to volunteer a little time. I feel loved and cared for even though essentially I am alone most of the time: Psalm 91:11 "For he will command his angels concerning you to guard you in all your ways." Now how much more can you ask than that?? God bless y'all. PS: Would love to see you at the Benefit on 03/31! It will give me a chance to thank you for your support and prayers!

Wakefield Cancer Update 04.01.12—What a wonderful time we had at my benefit. Seeing old friends, family, church family, regular family, and well isn't everybody just family? I was in tears numerous times. The benefit proceeds came up to $1989. I am just so touched and awed by everyone's support. $800 was from the raffle, around $1000 from the dinner and then other was direct support through mail. This will take a nice chunk out of the total amount owed ($10,000 after insurance). Insurance doesn't cover as much as it used to with high deductibles and maximum out of pockets. However, Keith and I are certainly blessed to have insurance, jobs, supportive family and friends. God has certainly been gracious to us. On another note, radiation treatments done, I am home, and pain is very minimal—what more could I ask? Not much. Love to you all! Is anyone interested in joining a thank-you-card-writing party???? Ha-ha. (I think I have around 80+ cards to write—but I am not complaining—no I'm not!!)

Wakefield Cancer Update—04.04.12 Okay, y'all are probably going to think I am a bit weird (well some of you know I am weird), but I am really excited at hair growth. While many women do all they can to get rid of some of their hair (in other places besides the head), I am excited to start seeing hair in those places AND my head AND my eyebrows AND my eyelashes. Yeah! I can actually see my eyebrows pretty well and my lashes are growing in nice and evenly. Head hair is now at 3/4 inch. Boy...if I would have thought I would be singing praises to God for less than an inch of hair...Life is fun! Laugh for the Day: God hasn't had to work too hard at counting the hairs in the last 6 months, but I am ready to put Him to work!!!!

04.17.12—I have to share my experience this last weekend. I had been planning for a month to attend the Ladies Day Apart in Derry, New Hampshire, with Karen Kingsbury, Christian author, as the speaker. This was my first outing since being diagnosed that did not have something to do with treatment, reaction to treatment, etc., so it was an exciting thing for me! Well I was riding with some friends that live in a town about 14 miles away. I decided to take the shortest route according to MapQuest. It was 4 in the morning and feeling very confident in my ability to follow directions off I go. Well the first direction that comes up that I am unfamiliar with takes me up someone's driveway. The next has a different name for the road than the road sign. The next is for a road that has no road sign. Well at this point, after making a call to my friends, is to continue on and hope for the best. At one point, I just keep driving down the road and come to a T. I get my Smart Phone out and try to get on to Navigator, and it freezes my phone up completely. So I pray, "Lord, you know I want to go today but if you have other plans, that is okay. If you want me to go, then you are going to have to get me to my friend's house because I have no idea where I am or which way to go." So I turn left, then right and just drive. After about 15 miles I come out to a kind-of-main road in the town I am headed for...cool, God, you got me this far. Now does my friend live this way or that way? I turn left and find the road that my friend lives off of. Okay Lord we are in business...you are too cool. I get to my friend's road with a few minutes to spare. It has been a few years since I had been there, so did not remember which driveway, so after going up 2 driveways that were obviously not hers, I finally reach my destination late by only 5 minutes. God is soooooo good. Great day in NH and wonderful fellowship with my friends.

Wakefield Cancer Update 04.17.12—Had appointment with oncologist this past Wednesday. Everything is looking good. We are a go for the 5-year aromatase inhibitor treatment (once-a-day pill). My cancer was estrogen-receptor which means this hormone will tend to encourage tumor development and progression, and so the inhibitor will lower the chance of this happening. We will have to see what side effects await with this treatment. Almost completely healed from the radiation treatment—just one small area, about the size of half a dime that is healing nicely and probably will take another week to heal completely. I will see the oncologist again in 6 weeks to check on my reaction to the drug and then in 6 months. Update to Benefit: Over $2000 total has come in and will be paying off 3 of my medical bills with that which will only leave 2 larger ones, both of which will have long-term payment arrangements made because of their size. Praise the Lord for His faithfulness.

Chapter 11

A Daughter's Perspective: Heather

I remember what a good day it had been out shopping for glasses with my mom and my sister, just spending time together. I had missed that when my mom and stepdad moved away to Arizona, so when they moved back to Maine, I was ecstatic. We tried to get together as much as we could on our days off, since we all had Mondays off from our respective jobs.

It started to gently sprinkle when we pulled into my sister Cassie's dooryard. We said our goodbyes, and I hopped in the front seat getting ready to be dropped off at my apartment. Then, my mom's phone rang before we even left the driveway. As soon as she started talking, I knew who it was. I saw a tear rolling down my mom's face and knew right then it was bad news.

I went back inside my sister's house to tell her she needed to come back out to the car. By then it was really raining. I remember the rain only because I was counting the raindrops as they hit the window while I was waiting for my mom to get off the phone so we could know what was going on, although in my heart, I already knew.

I don't remember how long the phone call was, but I remember trying not to cry as my mom told us the news. All I could think in my head was that I had to be strong; I had to not show my mom how much the news upset me. That didn't really happen. As ı as I would like to say I can keep my feelings to myself, the always written all over my face. I was worried. This was MY mom. How could this happen? My mom is the greatest woman I know. Why would something like this happen to her? I was sad, I was angry, I was pissed off. I had a swell of emotions that I can't put into words.

The conversation we had in the car is a blur. I don't think I could tell you what was said no matter how hard I try. I don't remember the ride home. I don't remember getting dropped off. I do remember sitting on my porch and crying for what seemed like forever. When I finally composed myself enough to go up to my apartment, and as soon as I saw my husband, the tears came all over again. I sobbed as I told him the news. He just held me as we stood in the kitchen. He knew all of the emotions I was having because he had dealt with it as well when he found out his mother had cancer.

I had to tell my son. I didn't want to say anything until we knew what was going on exactly. It was a very hard conversation to have. Kurt was a teenager, but he loves his family. The day I told him, he cried, we cried together. He asked questions about what was going to happen and I told him everything I knew. He was mature enough to understand. I don't know exactly what he was feeling because he tries to keep his feelings to himself most of the time, but I knew he was upset. I tried comforting him as much as I could, but with me being just as upset, I don't know how much comfort I actually was.

It seemed like everything was happening so fast. I wanted things to just slow down a little (even though I knew that they couldn't) just so I could process what was happening. The first thing I remember before anything actually started was a conversation I had with my mom on the phone and she said to me "All I can think is that I want my mom." Oh how I wish Nana could have been here to help sooth my mom's fears, just hold her and tell her everything would be okay, but because she wasn't with us anymore, it was now our jobs to see her through this.

We went to the first oncologist appointment. The oncologist gave us a run through of what could happen, but mom needed to see the surgeon before anything could be decided. I wasn't able to go to the surgeon's appointment with them because I had to work.

It was decided that she would have a double mastectomy. So next was surgery. During all of this I was having a lot of chest pain. I thought it was just the stress of it all. It got to the point where it was so bad I ended up in the emergency room.

Turns out my gallbladder needed to come out. Really? Now is when my body decides to do this? It couldn't have waited a year or so, or not happened at all? I had surgery a week before mom was scheduled to have her surgery. But no matter what, I was determined to be there when mom had her surgery.

My sister and I stayed at mom's house the night before surgery since we had to leave so early in the morning. Neither one of us slept. We tried, of course, but it did not come. My dad got home about two or three in the morning. We left around 4:30 a.m., if I remember correctly. I don't remember much about the drive to the hospital. I think it was just idle chatter, no one really wanting to talk about what was to come.

Mom got checked into the preop area. She was taken into a room away from us and we stayed in the waiting room. I remember mom's pastor coming and praying with my dad before her surgery. I remember thinking I didn't know too many people who would come to the hospital at six in the morning to pray before surgery. I was quite touched by the whole thing.

Mom was finally taken into surgery. I didn't see her but for a minute or two before she went in.

And then there was the wait. It seemed like days had gone by, the hours were dragging by so slowly. I remember being very uncomfortable in the waiting room, it was crowded and noisy, and being a week out from surgery myself, I couldn't get comfortable. Cassie and I got up to walk around and just waited.

My dad disappeared for a little while. We didn't know where he went. But then he came back, a decorative spider in hand. Mom loves tarantulas, so this was a good gift for her.

Finally, she was in a room. I remember she looked very tired. I don't remember much about the talks that we had while we were in the room. It was mostly mom asking us to make some phone calls for her and such. My dad went home because he had to tend to the dogs. I remember going to get some dinner at some point. I remember my mom's urine being blue because of the medication. It was quite the sight. My dad took a picture…you have to know my dad to understand that one.

I don't remember if it was the day of surgery or the following day, but I do remember mom having a reaction to not having breasts anymore. Of course in my eyes, she was my mom, I didn't see her any differently, but to be a woman and to lose something that is part of you, even if it is only flesh, it has to be hard.

Finally she could go home. I was so happy that she was home. Cassie and I took turns being at her house during her recovery while my dad was on the road. I hated seeing mom so incapacitated. Not that she was unable to do anything, because she was, but she looked weak and rundown. Surgery can do that to a person. I was so happy when I heard they could take the drains out finally and she could finish healing.

Chemotherapy was next. But before she started chemo, mom wanted to have a party. An "Unhairy Party" as she called it. A group of family and friends got together to play some games, eat some good food, the "bald deviled eggs" were my favorite and then came the shaving of heads.

Mom wanted to be in control of her own hair, so she decided instead of letting it fall out, she would shave it off. Not wanting her to be alone in the beauty of baldness, I decided I would shave my head with her. Who knew being bald would be so freeing? It was very emotional, not because I was losing my hair, because that was my choice. The emotional part was the reason mom was losing hers. Even though it was her choice to shave her head, it was the reason she had to that tore me apart.

So now we get to the chemotherapy. Every other Monday we went down so mom could get her chemo. At first, she'd have her chemo, we'd go to lunch and try to get some shopping done. That ended quickly. We soon learned that mom didn't have enough energy to do any shopping after chemo.

Chemo just seemed to take longer and longer. They had a hard time getting a blood return from her port, which set her back at least an hour, sometimes longer. Again, Cassie and I took turns staying with mom the week after chemo. Cassie would stay the beginning of the week. I'd go down on Wednesday and stay until Saturday usually, unless my dad got home before Saturday, then I'd come home earlier.

The first four sessions of chemo were hard. Mom didn't have an appetite at all. A few times we had to give her shots to help her white count. We, of course, didn't mind being there and caring for mom. It was just hard seeing her so uncomfortable, so tired. And on the days she forgot to take her nausea medication at the right time, she just couldn't seem to get a hold on it and felt like crap the next couple of days.

I remember throughout the chemotherapy process I got sick twice, so I wasn't able to stay with mom. Cassie would stay longer, and it just so happened that my dad came home early those weeks. Funny how that happens, huh?

It's Thanksgiving day, and I was sick. I had to wear a mask, so I didn't give any germs to mom.

The second half of chemotherapy was hard on mom. She didn't have the nausea or loss of appetite anymore. Now she had bone pain and weakness. I remember how stubborn she could be. She fell while I was there once. I was outside with the dog and on the phone with my husband. Do you think she yelled for me to come help her? Of course not.

She said, "Well what would I have done if you weren't here?" Well, I was there, and I was there to help! I was a little angry that she didn't think she should yell for me to help her. I got over it of course.

Finally, chemo was over. It took sixteen weeks. Looking back, even though it was a crappy time, it was still time I got to spend with my mom, time that was given to us and I cherished every moment I could.

The next step was radiation. We moved mom to The Arbor House the weekend before her radiation therapy was to start. They graciously let her stay there the six and a half weeks because she lived so far away. I didn't get to visit her much while she was there. I didn't have a car at the time. When I did get a car finally, she was almost done radiation. Cassie and I took our children up to see her one day, so we could spend some time together. We went out to lunch, talked, had fun. It was nice to see her in better spirits.

Then the radiation started to rear its ugly head. My mom is very fair skinned, so we wondered how bad the burns were going to be. I never thought they would be as bad as they got. I can't imagine what pain that must have been.

I remember the color of the burns. They weren't red like you would think they would be. They were black, blue and purple. I told my husband about them one day and he couldn't believe it. I had snapped a picture of them, so I could prove just how bad they were.

Finally, it is over! Yay! No more chemo, no more radiation. Finally, Mom can get back to her life.

I have to say what surprised me most about the journey was the outpouring of love and support mom received. I expected people to reach out, but I guess I never realized how many people would.

We had a benefit for mom to help her with paying the medical expenses that insurance didn't cover. It was a good day. A lot of people showed up and it was just all around a great showing of how many people truly support my mom. It was very endearing.

The journey my mom was taking was an emotional roller-coaster, and it was for me as well. I don't think I ever really dealt with my feelings about mom having cancer or about how scared I was. I'm more of a fixer and want to take control of the situation and make sure things get done when they need to.

I took on that role as much as I could and as much as other people would let me, so I kind of back-burnered my own feelings. But they always came back to bite me in the butt. I'd be in the shower and just start sobbing. At night when I couldn't sleep, my emotions would overwhelm me. I tried to not cry in front of my mom. Sometimes I couldn't help it, but it wasn't very often. I didn't want her to worry about how I was dealing with things because she had enough on her plate. I don't remember ever thinking my mom would die, but the pure fact that she was going through this and there was nothing I could do to take her pain away overwhelmed me.

What I am most awed by is mom's strength. It was always there, even when she didn't see it. Her strength throughout gave me strength.

Chapter 12

A Daughter's Perspective: Casandra

The day I found out my mom had breast cancer was a hard day. The emotions that ran through my head were overwhelming. I was angry that they told her over the phone, sad that she had to deal with this, worried that she was going to die, and stressed that I wouldn't be able to help her and still work. As all these things were going on in my head I also had to be strong. I automatically went into caregiver mode, saying we had to find out everything, make appointments and take it step by step.

After my mom left and I was alone I broke down. I was really scared, imagining the worst.

We went to the Dempsey Center and they were so helpful and letting us know we could always go there for support and help. It was amazing. Heather, Toby and I went to a luncheon with other caregivers and listened to a special speaker and got some great information on how to handle all the information from all the doctors and surgeons.

As we found out what kind of cancer she had and the options that were available, it became a little easier, not much, but we had a name and a stage. Mom had the option to have one breast removed and then maybe get plastic surgery for a new one later down the road.

I really had mixed feelings when she decided to have both breasts removed and didn't want plastic surgery.

She said, "I'm older and am not worried about having breasts."

I thought to myself, "How can she want that? Maybe she just wants to get it over with. Maybe she's just being hasty." Then I realized that this is me thinking as a woman; I don't think I could live with no breasts. She was firm and confident with her decision and she reassured me it was truly what she wanted.

The surgery to have her breasts removed was long. Waiting for it brought back all those emotions like when we found out in the beginning. Plus, I'm always so worried when someone goes under anesthesia, especially with my mom because she has a rough time coming out from under it.

When we finally found out everything went well a weight lifted. I was still sad to see part of her missing, but I was so happy everything went well. My mom was such a trooper and was barely in the hospital for two days. Amazing!

Heather and I worked out a schedule; I would be there to take care of her the first half of the week, and she would do the latter.

It was hard to see her without her clothes on. The stitches and scars and let's not even talk about the drainage tubes that had to stay half in her body and half out to get the fluid out. I'm glad mom drained them herself most of the time. It was so gross. The color and clots really made me queasy.

I think she healed pretty well and about a month later she went to get her port placed. That was just a day surgery, so it wasn't as tough as the double mastectomy. A couple of weeks later chemotherapy started. Chemotherapy was hard. Sitting beside her watching this poison being put into her, she looked broken some days, tired, exhausted, and drained. As a caregiver and family member, sometimes it was hard to take care of her, I mean she's my mom, she took care of me. Sometimes it was a little hard, when having to make sure she ate and took her meds even when she didn't want to.

I was so proud of her. Through everything she barely missed any work. To be honest I was a little jealous, because I missed a lot of work. Don't get me wrong, I wanted to be there every step and every appointment, and I felt horrible when I couldn't. But sometimes I would stay home just to get my emotions in check; mostly crying the day away. It's not because I had to care for her, it was that she had to be going through this and I don't know, I guess you don't know how it's going to turn out until everything's done, and the doctor says four wonderful words: "You are cancer free."

I think the worst part of everything for me was the radiation, only because I couldn't be with her a lot of the time and she was in excruciating pain and there was nothing I could do. It was hard, as I said earlier, to see her with no breasts and her chest sucked in, but seeing her after a couple weeks of radiation was even worse. Her skin looked like it had third- and fourth-degree burns on it. She couldn't put her arm down without wincing. But she pulled through that too.

Now she is cancer free and I really hope it stays that way. My mom is my hero and I'm so proud to be her daughter, even though she's a pain in the butt sometimes!!! Love you mom!

Epilogue

It has been approximately five years since I have touched this story. During that time, I continued with follow-up visits with the oncologist and am considered to have "no evidence of disease."

I did have another detour when I suffered a seizure and had to go through a thorough workup to determine its cause, to find out ultimately that I have a seizure disorder and not related to the cancer. I am on medicine and have only had that one seizure. Otherwise, I am just getting older and experiencing physical aspects of the natural aging process.

In April 2016, Keith, the love of my life, became very ill with a rare pulmonary disease and spent four months in a hospital, ultimately passing away on August 30, 2016.

I now live in Florida with Heather and her husband Rick. He is a teacher and a high school football coach. She works from home as a medical biller. I still work from home for a national medical transcription company.

I am not sure why God had me take a few other detours on my documentation journey, but then God said, "Now is the time."

Oftentimes we know him more intimately through the bumps in the road, the back trails of uncertainty and the 4-lane highways of bumper-to-bumper traffic. I initially felt that by putting my story in writing, it would be an encouragement to at least one person who might read it as well as an important memorial to God's faithfulness in the midst of the storm. I do not know what God's plan is for it.

Perhaps it was just for me. I just need to be obedient in the doing and leave the rest up to him.

My journey was to Breast Cancer, Maine. Your journey may take you somewhere else like Heart Attack, Oklahoma. Still another might be headed to Bankruptcy, Vermont. I know of some who have taken a detour to COPD, California, and Bipolar, Alabama. No matter where our journeys take us, we all deal with the same realities: Questions, frustrations, hurt, physical and emotional pain, discouragement, worry, and a host of other emotions and perhaps physical ailments that interrupt our living and become a tangible milestone that make up the entirety of our existence.

For me, I cannot imagine any of life's journey, whether seemingly pleasant or unpleasant, without the presence of Jesus Christ, my God and my Savior. Without him, I could do nothing, I am nothing. I hope that if you are seeking something to give your life meaning, that you will seek the someone, the only one, who makes life worth living and brings living to life.

May God bless you.

About the Author

Terri Wakefield currently resides in Sebastian, Florida, with one of her daughters and son-in-law, Heather and Rick, along with two rescue cats named Boo and Mischief. She has five children (Casandra, Jennie, Heather, Liz, and Toby) and eighteen grandchildren. She was born and raised in Maine but has also spent a few years living in California, Vermont, Minnesota, and Arizona. Terri loves to read, bake, and paint. She works as a production manager in a national medical transcription service and has worked as a medical transcriptionist, medical editor and proofreader, church secretary, and administrative secretary. Terri has also ministered as a lay Christian counselor and has taught Sunday School and Bible studies. She enjoyed a wonderful marriage to her late husband Keith and misses his laughter and joy and companionship. Alongside him, she served as a domestic missionary in a Christ-centered treatment program for troubled teens.

Terri accepted Jesus as her Lord and Savior as a teenager (nearly fifty years ago) and has had a life-long relationship with God and continues to experience God's glorious grace and blessings in good times and in challenging ones. She has a passion to share God's love and faithfulness to struggling Christians, so they too can experience the fullness of a relationship with him throughout life's journey here on earth.

CPSIA information can be obtained
at www.ICGtesting.com
Printed in the USA
BVHW09s2145031018
529256BV00013B/66/P